OCS Study
MMS 2005-031

Climatology of Ocean Features in the Gulf of Mexico

Final Report

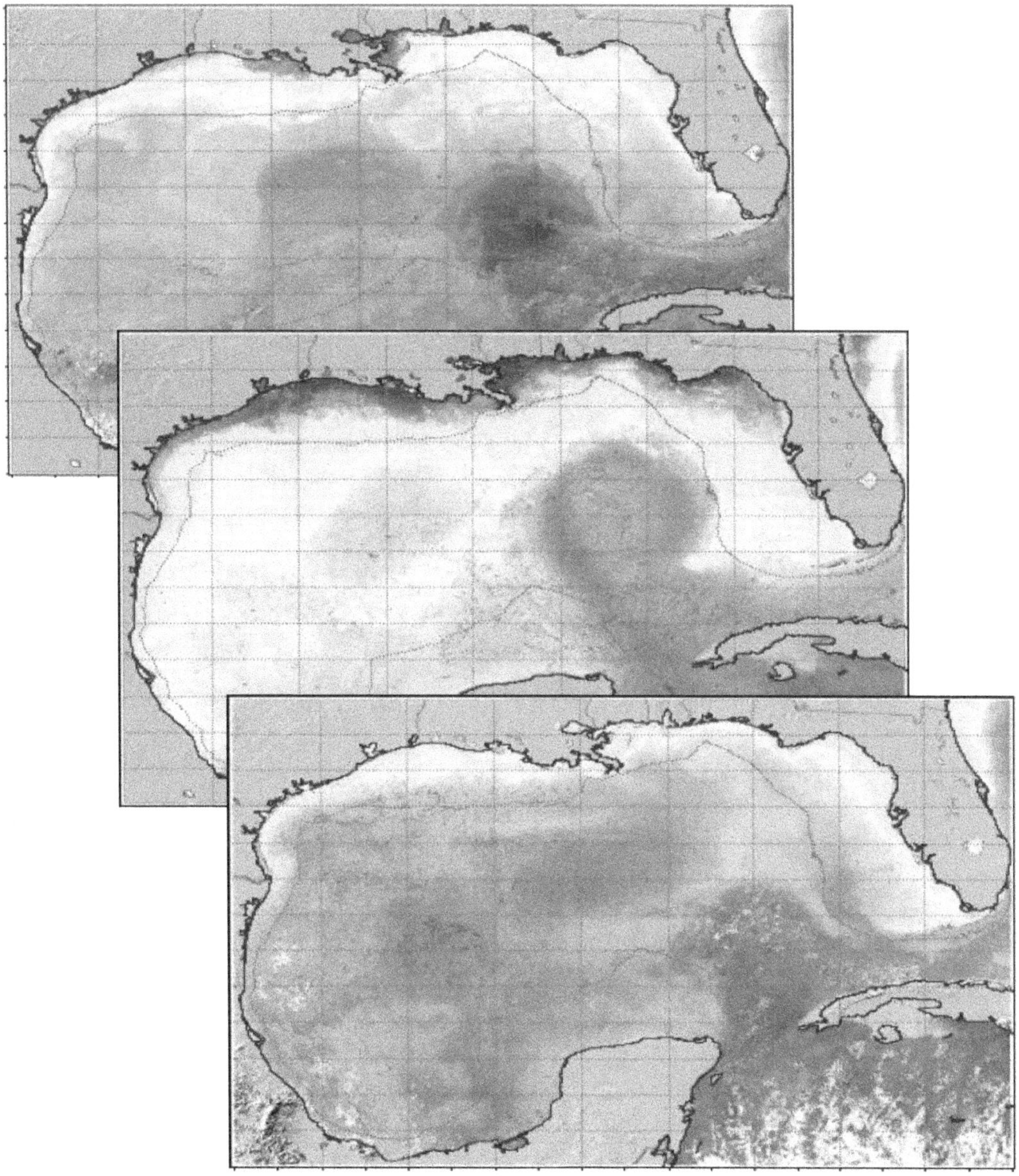

MMS U.S. Department of the Interior
Minerals Management Service
Gulf of Mexico OCS Region

OCS Study
MMS 2005-031

Climatology of Ocean Features in the Gulf of Mexico

Final Report

Author

Fred M. Vukovich

Prepared under MMS Contract
1435-01-03-PO-74302
by
Science Applications International Corporation
615 Oberlin Rd., Suite 100
Raleigh, North Carolina 27587

Published by

U.S. Department of the Interior
Minerals Management Service
Gulf of Mexico OCS Region

New Orleans
June 2005

DISCLAIMER

This report was prepared under contract between the Mineral Management Service (MMS) and Science Applications International Corporation (SAIC). This report has been technically reviewed by MMS and approved for publication. Approval does not signify that the contents necessarily reflect the views and polices of MMS, nor does mention of trade names or commercial products constitute endorsement or recommendation for use. It is, however, exempt from review and compliance with the MMS editorial standards.

REPORT AVAILABILITY

Extra copies of this report may be obtained from Public Information Office (Mail Stop 5034) at the following address:

U.S. Department of the Interior
Minerals Management Service
Gulf of Mexico OCS Region
Public Information Office (MS 5034)
1201 Elmwood Park Blvd.
New Orleans, LA 70123-2394

Telephone Number: 1-504-736-2519 or
1-800-200-GULF

CITATION

Suggested citation:

Vukovich, F.M., 2005. Climatology of Ocean Features in the Gulf of Mexico: Final Report. U.S. Department of the Interior, Minerals Management Service, Gulf of Mexico OCS Region, New Orleans, LA. OCS Study MMS 2005-031 58 pp.

ABOUT THE COVER

The cover picture shows a series of NOAA/AVHR SST images depicting warm core rings that separated from the Loop Current in the Gulf of Mexico in 1997, 1998, and 1999.

ABSTRACT

The objective of this project is to develop a climatology of certain ocean features in the Gulf of Mexico (GOM) using data sets that span long time periods (i.e., as long as 32 years in some cases) to create the statistics. Twelve (12) separate statistics were created, some of which described characteristics of the Loop Current, while others were involved with warm core eddies that separate from the Loop Current and cold core eddies. The data resources used to create this climatology included analyzed in-situ data from ships of opportunity, from field programs in the GOM, and from the projects managed by the various oil and gas companies. However, the principal data used for this study were satellite remote sensing data, which included sea-surface temperature data from radiometers aboard TIROS-M, HCMM, SEASAT, and the numerous NOAA polar orbiting satellites; ocean color data from the CZCS, which was aboard the Nimbus polar orbiting satellite, SeaWiFS, and MODIS; and altimeter data from the TOPEX/Poseiden and the ERS instruments. These data were used to develop ocean front analyses in the GOM, which provided the "characteristic" position of the fronts for a given month. It is expected that these statistics will be useful in planning field programs, to marine biologists, to oceanographers, as background information for environmental impact statements (EISs), in evaluating and directing improvements for models that calculate the ocean dynamics in the GOM, and for oil and gas operations in the GOM.

ACKNOWLEDGMENTS

The author wishes to thank Dr. Carole Current, the MMS Contracting Officer's Technical Representative, and Dr. Alexis Lugo-Fernandez for their continuing support of this project. I would also like to thank the people, too numerous to cite, who contributed information and data that helped create the continuous datasets from which many of the statistics cited in this report were derived.

TABLE OF CONTENTS

LIST OF FIGURES

LIST OF FIGURES (continued)

LIST OF TABLES

1. EXECUTIVE SUMMARY

1.1 Objective and Data

The objective of this project is to develop a climatology of certain ocean features in the Gulf of Mexico (GOM) using data sets that span long time periods (i.e., as long as 32 years in some cases) to create the statistics. The climatology focused on three principal ocean features: the Loop Current (LC); warm core rings (WCRs); and cold core rings (CCRs). Twelve (12) separate statistics were created. Four of these twelve statistics dealt with aspects of the LC; that is, the spatial frequency with which the LC is found in the eastern GOM (EGOM), the frequency of the orientation angle of the LC, the spatial frequency with which isolated pockets of warm LC water are found in the EGOM, and the spatial frequency with which isolated pockets of warm LC water are found on the West Florida Shelf. A major portion of the effort focused on WCRs. Seven separate statistics were created for WCRs; that is, the dominant frequency of separation of WCRs from the LC, which was examined using two separate statistics, the frequency with which WCRs move along certain paths as they move through the western GOM (WGOM) to the western wall, WCRs' speeds as they traverse across the WGOM, the mean decay of the WCR size as they move through the WGOM, the spatial frequency with which WCR water is found in the WGOM, and the spatial frequency with which the centers of WCRs water are found in the GOM. Only one statistic could be created about CCRs. CCRs are short-lived phenomena compared to the lifetime of WCR. They are much more difficult to detect in satellite remote sensing data other than altimetry data. Their motion is very often associated with the LC or with WCRs. The statistic that was created for CCRs is the spatial frequency with which the centers of CCRs are found in the GOM. This report describes the procedures used to create the statistics and relates the statistics to known processes in the GOM.

The data resources used to create this climatology included analyzed in-situ data from ships of opportunity, from MMS field programs in the GOM, and from GOM projects managed by the various oil and gas companies. The bulk of the information was, however, obtained from satellite remote sensing data. These data included sea-surface temperature (SST) data from radiometers aboard TIROS-M, HCMM, SEASAT, GOES, and the numerous NOAA polar orbiting satellites; ocean color data from the CZCS, which was aboard the Nimbus polar orbiting satellite, and from the SeaWiFS system; and altimeter data from the TOPEX/Poseiden and the ERS systems. These data were used to develop monthly ocean front analyses in the GOM from which many of the statistics were derived. These analyses were created using an integral of available satellite clear-sky images (i.e., satellite SST, ocean color, and altimetry imagery) and of any available information and/or analyzed in-situ data obtained in a particular month. The LC front was the approximate average front for the month unless a WCR separated from the LC during that month. In that case, it is the position of front after separation had occurred. WCR fronts were the approximate average front for the month. As a result, these analyses provided the "characteristic" position of the fronts in the GOM for a given month.

The development of the front analyses was based, for the most part, on satellite remote sensing data. In the periods 1976 through 1978 and 1986 through 1991, only SST data

1

were available to create the ocean front analysis in the GOM. Most of the SST data were obtained from the NOAA/AVHRR, though significant use was also made of GOES SST and SST data from NASA's Heat Capacity Mapping Mission (HCMM). As a result of using only SST data in the periods mentioned above, the frontal analyses could only be determined for as little as 5 months and as many as 8 months in a year, depending on when the mixed layer developed in the summer and was removed in the autumn. However, in those periods when satellite SST data were not useful, significant use was made of "ship-of opportunity" data to fill data gaps in climatological data sets for certain ocean features (e.g., position of the northern boundary of the LC, the location of WCRs, the month in which separation of a WCR from the LC occurred, etc). In the period 1979 through 1985, CZCS ocean color data were used to supplement the SST data, which were used to detect ocean features in the warm season when SST data were of little use. After 1991, TOPEX/ERS SSH data were available and the frontal analyses for most features could be developed for each month in the year. After 1997, SeaWiFS ocean color data were also used to supplement the SST data in the warm season to detect features that could not be detected in the SSH data (e.g., intrusions of LC water on the WFS). However, only limited amounts of these data were available for analysis because of the commercial nature of the SeaWiFS data.

It is expected that these statistics will be useful in planning field programs, to marine biologists and oceanographers, as background information for environmental impact statements (EISs), in evaluating and directing improvements for models that calculate the ocean dynamics, and for oil and gas exploration and exploitation in the GOM.

The following sections provide examples of the statistics that have been developed.

1.2. Frequency of Loop Current Water in the EGOM

The LC frontal boundary (Figure 1.1) seldom reached the 28° latitude line (i.e., about 5% of the time over the 28-year period of the statistic). It reached the 27° latitude line about 20% of the time. The LC usually penetrates at least as far north as 27° N latitude just prior to WCR separation. After WCR separation, the LC re-establishes itself further south, usually at around 25° latitude, so that it does not normally occupy the northern part of the EGOM (i.e., north of 25 °N) for long periods of time. The water mass associated with the LC occupied the region south of 24° N latitude and east of 86° W longitude the greatest amount of time. The analysis suggests that the LC was at times found on the Yucatan shelf and the West Florida Shelf. There are cases when LC thermal boundary that was found in the satellite SST imagery and in the ocean color imagery were found on these shelves. This, of course, does not mean that the high-speed currents associated with the LC were found on either shelf. The analysis shows that there is a mean westward tilt (i.e., a westward tilt of approximately 30°) of the axis of the LC.

1.3 Frequency of Loop Current Water on the West Florida Shelf

The analysis of the spatial frequency of warm LC water on the West Florida shelf (WFS) shows that intrusions of LC water onto the shelf occurred most often south of 27° N and between the 200-m isobath and the 83° W longitude line (Figure 1.2); that is, most of these intrusions occurred near the shelf break and do not penetrate deep into the shelf (i.e., they do not penetrate deep into the shelf as an identifiable features in the satellite remote sensing data). The inability to detect deep penetration of these features on the

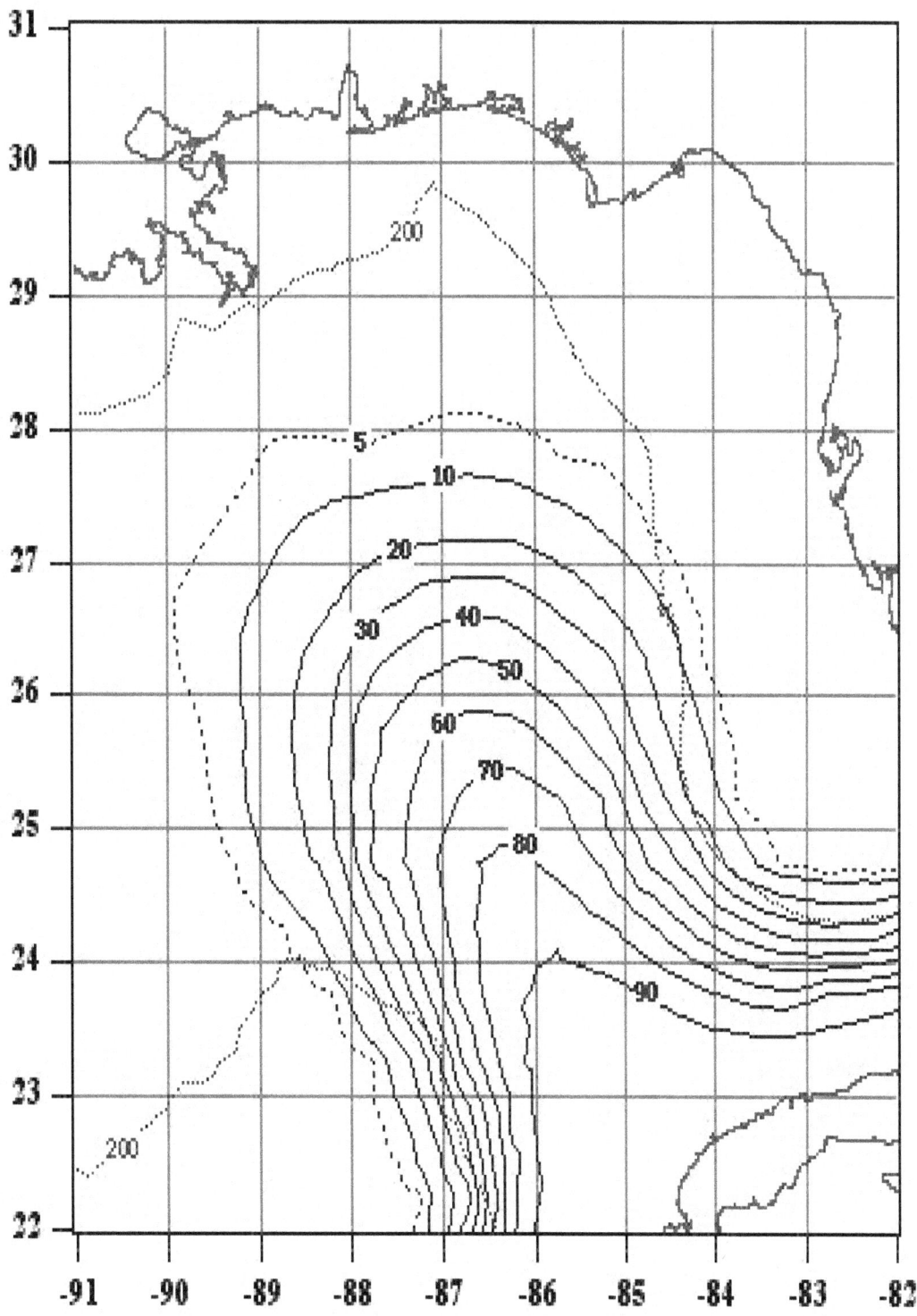

Figure 1.1. Spatial frequency (%) of the water mass associated with the LC in the EGOM based on data for the period 1976-2003.

3

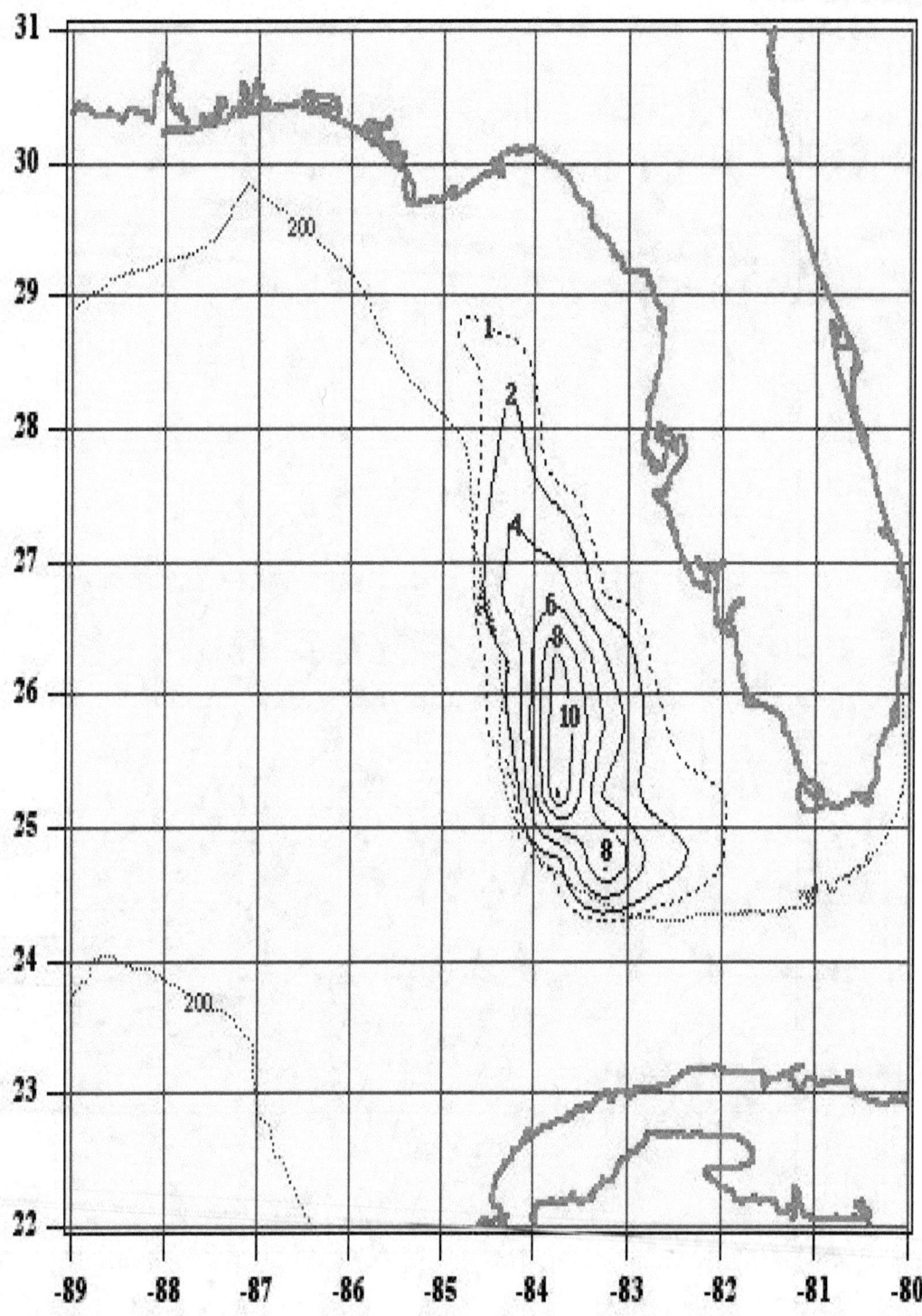

Figure 1.2. Spatial frequency (%) of LC water on the West Florida Shelf based on data for the period 1976-2003.

shelf using satellite remote sensing data is presumably due to mixing, which causes shelf water to become indistinguishable from LC water. It also appears that the intrusions of LC water onto the shelf occurs most often when a CCR, whose circulation causes the transport, is located on the southeastern portion of the LC front near the Dry Tortugas. The maximum spatial frequency for these events is about 12%, which correspond to a frequency of about 1 event every year.

1.4 Frequency of the Position of WCR Centers in the GOM

The analysis (Figure 1.3) shows an east-west zone of relatively high spatial frequency for the ring centers located in the 25° N-26° N latitude belt from 88° W to 94° W. Multiple centers are found in that zone, and the maximum frequency in that zone is about 12%, which is a little more than one event every year, on average. One event every year might be considered rather high considering that major rings do not necessarily separate from the LC that often nor is the path of the rings always in this area. There are a couple of reasons for this frequency. As shown in this report, during periods when the movement of major rings slowed because they were either changing direction or their motion formed a loop, the ring, in some case, did not move over a great distance and occupied the same grid square for more than a one-month period. Another reason for the one event every year frequency is the fact that minor rings were included in the analysis. Minor rings move slowly, are often quasi-stationary, and dissipate quickly. Under these conditions, minor rings can made a serious contribution in the analysis.

North of the eastern part of the east-west zone of relatively high frequency is a secondary center of relatively high spatial frequency for the ring centers (i.e., located at around 27.5° N and 89.5° W). The maximum frequency in this center is about 7%, which is about one event every 17 months. In this region, minor rings made serious contributions to the spatial frequency. This center is important because rings located in this region can make a marked impact on the circulation on the Texas-Louisiana shelf and the slope in that region, which will impact outer continental shelf activities in that region.

Immediately west of the east-west zone of relatively high frequency is a center of relatively low spatial frequency (i.e., located at around 25.5° N and 94.5° W). The minimum frequency in that center is about 3%, which is about one event every 4 years. The reason for the minimum in this region is not completely clear. Data provided in this report indicate that this area is an area where CCRs are often found. The dominance of CCRs in this region may inhibit WCRs from invading the region. WCRs are normally much smaller when they reach the western wall of the WGOM and have about the same dimensions as CCRs in this area, so that a CCR is just as likely to occupy a position near the western wall as a WCR. The data on ring path provided in the report would suggests that very few major rings move into this region when they traverse the WGOM to the western wall.

North and south of the minimum area discussed in the last paragraph are areas of relatively high frequency for ring centers. The area to the north is in the northwestern corner of the GOM, which region has been called the "graveyard for rings." Rings have been observed to reside in this area for long periods of time; and at times, those rings have become revitalized for a period of time due to interactions with other WCRs (Vukovich and Waddell, 1991) and/or with CCRs. The maximum frequency in that area is about 10%, which is about one event every year.

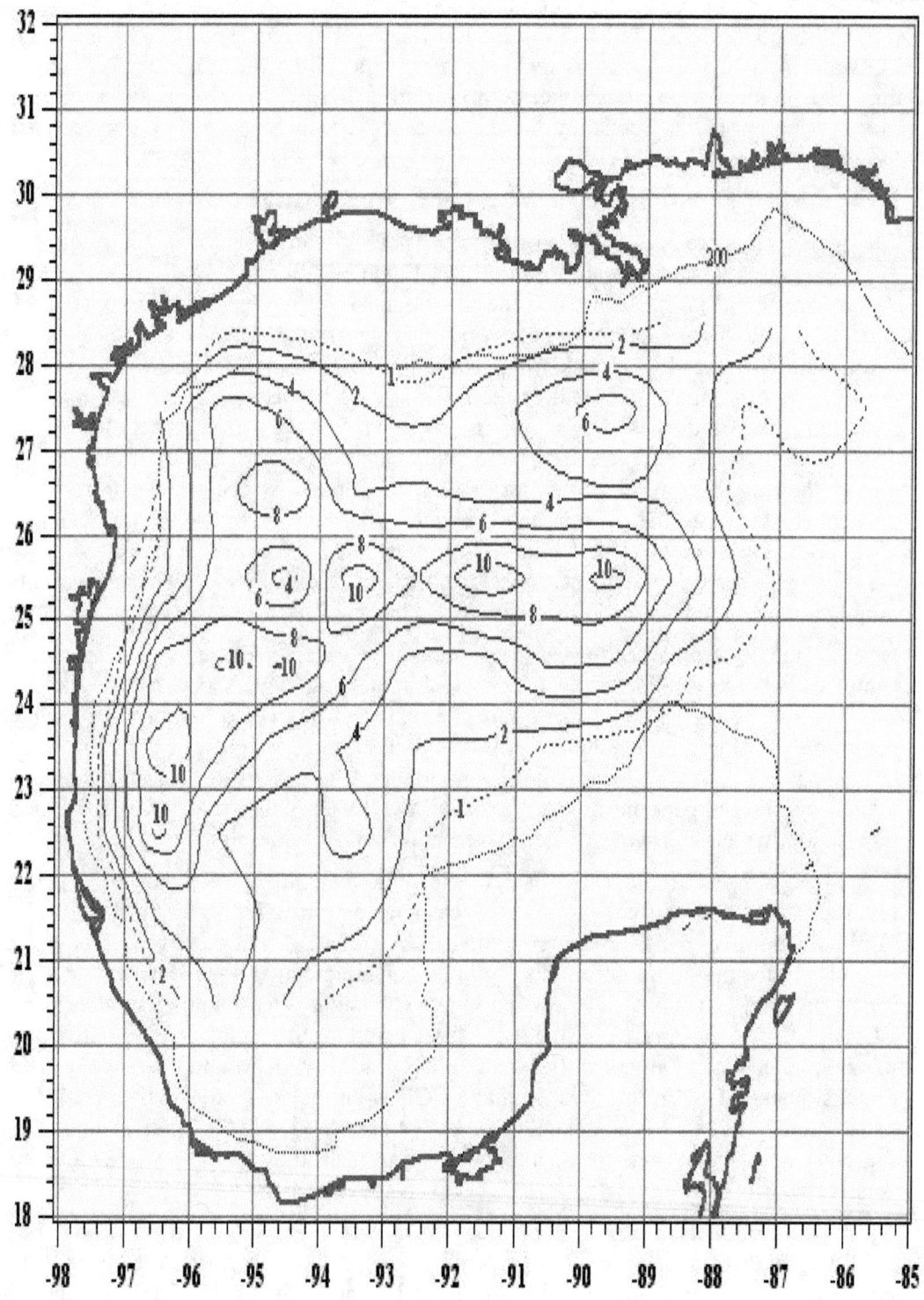

Figure 1.3. Spatial frequency (%) for the location of WCR centers using a 27-year (1977-2003) database.

The zone of relatively high frequency in the area to the south of the minimum area is located near the western boundary of the GOM and the maximum frequency in that area is about 12%, which is a little greater than one event every year. The fact that there is a persistence of WCR centers in this area supports the notion that these rings are major contributors to the transport in the WGOM and the maintenance of an anticyclonic cell along the western boundary of the GOM (Brooks, 1984; Nowlin and McLellan, 1967; Elliott 1982).

1.5 Summary of Findings

The following is an outline of the major findings from this study:

Loop Current

The LC front reached 28° N latitude in the EGOM only about 5% of the time and 27° N about 20% of the time. About 80% of the LC's orientation angles are between 0° (a north-south orientation) and 30° (a north-northwest to south-southeast orientation), which represent a stable orientation for the LC; that is, ring separation is not expected anytime soon. Less than 20% of the LC's orientation angles are greater than 30°, which represent an unstable mode for the LC and ring separation is usually expected soon.

Isolated warm pools of LC water were found throughout the region north of 26° N in the EGOM. The highest frequency for the warm pools in the EGOM was about 14% and it was found near 27° N and 85° W, just west of the shelf break for the WFS. This center of high frequency was created, for the most part, as a result of many cases in which there was transport of warm LC water by the circulation associated with CCRs located on the boundary of the LC.

Intrusions of LC water onto the WFS are, for the most part, due to transport associated with a CCR located on the eastern boundary of the LC. Most of these intrusions are found south of 27° N and between the shelf break and 83° W. The maximum frequency is about 12%, which corresponds to about one event per year.

Warm Core Rings

The frequency distribution for the period for separation of major rings from the LC had a bi-model distribution with modes at 6 and 11 months and a range of 5 to 19 months. The average period was 11 months and the standard deviation was ± 4 months. The average period was identical to one of the modes of the frequency distribution, suggesting that 11 months might be the most characteristic period for eddy shedding. The average period did not change substantially over the 10-year period 1994-2003, remaining at about 11 months. A high frequency of ring separation was found in March, and no rings were observed to separate from the LC in December.

The period with the most significant variance in the variance-preserved spectrum of the LC northern boundary variations was 12 months, suggesting that 12 months might be the most characteristic period for eddy shedding based on these data. The most significant variance showed a one-month variation over the last ten years (1994-2003), presumably a result of the year-to-year variability in the eddy-shedding period.

In terms of the path that the WCRs take through the WGOM, the Central Path had the highest frequency (62%). The Northern Path had the next highest frequency (24%), and the least likely trajectory for the WCRs was the Southern Path (18%). The average speed of the WCRs through the WGOM was 4.4 km/day with a standard deviation of ± 2.9 km/day. The frequency distribution of WCR speeds had a bi-model distribution with modes in the increments of 4.0 to 4.9 km/day and 1.0 to 1.9 km/day.

WCRs decayed, on average, to about 55% of their initial size in about 8 months. There was a period of about two months, starting at the fourth month after separation of the ring, when the decay rate decreased significantly.

The maximum frequency of WCR water in the WGOM occurred near 25°N and 90° W and was 24%. There was a zone of relatively high frequency of WCR water in the WGOM that stretched along a west-southwest--east-northeast line from 26° N and 90° W to 24.75° N and 95° W where the frequency varied from 24% to 16%, which appeared to be associated with the Central Path of the major rings through the WGOM. The frequency contours for WCR water ridged into the northwest corner of the WGOM where major WCRs are often observed.

An east-west zone of relatively high frequency of WCRs was found in the WGOM in the 25-26° N latitude belt from 88° W to 94° W in which the maximum frequency was about 12%, corresponding to little more than one event per year. A secondary region of relatively high frequency of WCRs was found at around 27.4° N and 89.6° W for which minor rings played a significant role. Another region of relatively high frequency of WCR was found in the northwest corner of the WGOM, where, as previously indicated, major rings are often observed. Another region of relatively high frequency of WCRs was found near the western wall between 22° N and 25° N, in which the maximum frequency was about 12%, corresponding to little more than one event per year. This region supports the notion that WCRs may be major contributors to transport in the WGOM and the maintenance of an anticyclonic cell along the GOM's western boundary (Brooks, 1984; Nowlin and McLellan, 1967; Elliott 1982). In the WGOM, WCRs play an important role in the heat and salt balance (Elliot, 1982). These data indicate that WCRs have their most significant effect on the heat and salt balance north of 24° N.

Cold Core Rings

In the EGOM, there was a northwest-southeast oriented zone of relatively high frequency for CCRs, having two centers of maximum. The northwestern center was located at around 27.5° N and 88.5° W, which is in an area where CCRs have been previously found to intensify and/or develop (Vukovich, 1988a), and the maximum frequency in this area was about 30% (the highest frequency noted for any kind of ring—warm or cold), which corresponds to about 3-4 events per year. The southeastern center was located at around 25.5° N and 85.5° W, which is in the Dry Tortugas region where CCRs have been previously noted (Maul and Herman, 1985 and Vukovich 1988a and b), and the maximum frequency in this area was about 17%, which corresponds to about 2 events per year. In the WGOM, four region of relatively high frequency for CCRs were found. The maximum frequency in these regions varied from 16-20%, corresponding to about 1-2 events per year.

This study showed that in the EGOM, CCRs, which are very persistent and/or numerous in that region, play an important role in redistributing heat and salt. They accounted for a large portion of the development of isolated pools LC water in the EGOM and for all intrusions of LC water onto the WFS through transport associated with their circulation.

2. INTRODUCTION

In the late 1980s, a climatology (Vukovich and Hamilton, 1990) of a limited number of oceanographic features in the Gulf of Mexico (GOM) was created that was based on satellite remote sensing and in-situ data. Other aspects of the climatology of features in the GOM have been subsequently reported in the literature over the years (Vukovich, 1995; Vukovich; 1988a; Herring et al., 1997; Vukovich et al., 1978 and 1979b; Vukovich et al., 1979a; Sturges, 1992; Sturges, 1995; Sturges and Leben, 2000; Jacobs and Leben, 1990). Among the features included in those studies were the frequency of Loop Current (LC) water in the eastern GOM, LC eddy separation periods, cold core rings (CCRs) on the LC boundary, and warm core ring (WCR) water in the GOM. Up to 28 years of data were used in at least one of those studies. Most, however, used datasets that had much smaller periods (i.e., about 10-15 years, on average). The data set that is available to develop a climatology of oceanographic features in the GOM now span up to 32 years, which would lend greater statistical significance to the climatology. Furthermore, it is possible to develop additional statistics that were previously unattainable because the required data were not available. It is the objective of this project to develop the most up-to-date and statistical significance climatology possible of certain ocean features in the GOM.

The statistics on which this climatology is based on, are as follows:

1. Spatial frequency of Loop Current water in the Eastern GOM (EGOM). [Database period: 1976-2003];

2. Spatial frequency of warm water associated with major WCRs in the Western GOM (WGOM). [Database period: 1977-2003]

3. Spatial frequency of centers of WCRs in the WGOM (based on the location of the centers of both major and minor WCRs). [Database period: 1977-2003]

4. Frequency of the path of major WCRs in the WGOM (based on three potential ring-path subdivisions—the northern path, central path, and southern path). [Database period: 1976-2003]

5. Frequency of the speed of major WCRs in the Western GOM [Database period: 1972-2003]

6. Mean decay of the size of the major WCRs (Ring Dissipation) [Database period: 1976-2003]

7. Frequency of major eddy shedding periods from the LC. [Database period: 1972-2003]

8. Periods of oscillation of the LC's Northern Boundary. [Database period: 1977-2003]

9. Frequency of the orientation of the LC. [Database period: 1976-2003]

10. Spatial frequency of LC water in the EGOM not directly associated with the LC or with major WCRs (This water mass is, for the most part, associated with minor WCRs and with the advection of warm LC water by cold core rings [CCRs]). [Database period: 1976-2003]

11. Spatial frequency of intrusions of LC water onto the West Florida shelf (WFS). [Database period: 1976-2203]

12. Spatial frequency of centers of CCRs in the GOM. [Database period: 1992-2003]

The data resources used to create this climatology included analyzed in-situ data from ships of opportunity and from various MMS field programs in the GOM; information from the GOM programs managed by the various oil and gas companies; sea-surface temperature (SST) data from radiometers aboard TIROS-M, HCCM, SEASAT, GOES, and the numerous NOAA polar orbiting satellites; ocean color data from the CZCS, which was aboard the NIMBUS polar orbiting satellite, SeaWiFS, and MODIS; and altimeter data from the TOPEX/Poseiden and the ERS instruments. The application of the data from these sources to develop each statistic is discussed in the report.

It is hoped that the information that is derived from this integrated climatology may be useful in planning field programs, to marine biologists and oceanographers, as background information for environmental impact statements (EISs), and for oil and gas exploration and exploitation in the GOM. It has also been shown that the information from a climatology of ocean can useful in evaluating and directing improvements for models that calculate the ocean dynamics in the GOM (Herring et al., 1997). In the following sections of this report, a description of the steps that were taken to create the various statistics and a description of the features of each of the derived statistics are presented.

3. ANALYSIS OF FRONTS IN THE GOM

The principal data set used to derive many of the statistics that are presented in this report, are monthly analyses of the fronts in the GOM. These analyses provide the "characteristic" position of the fronts in the GOM for a given month. They were created using an integral of available satellite clear-sky images (i.e., satellite SST, ocean color, and altimetry imagery) and of any available information on ocean features and/or analyzed in-situ data for the month in question in the GOM. The LC front is the approximate average front for the month unless a WCR separated from the LC during that month. In that case, it is the position of front after separation has occurred. WCR fronts are the approximate average front for the month. If isolated pools of warm LC water not directly associated with the LC or with major WCRs are found in the EGOM in a given month, then it is represented in the frontal analysis by its most widespread effect in the EGOM for that month that is found in the available data resources. If an intrusion of warm LC water onto the WFS is found in the EGOM in a given month, then it is also represented by the most widespread effect for that month on that shelf that is found in the available data resources. These frontal analyses have been created for the period 1976-2003. Figure 3.1 is an example of a frontal analysis used to derive statistics.

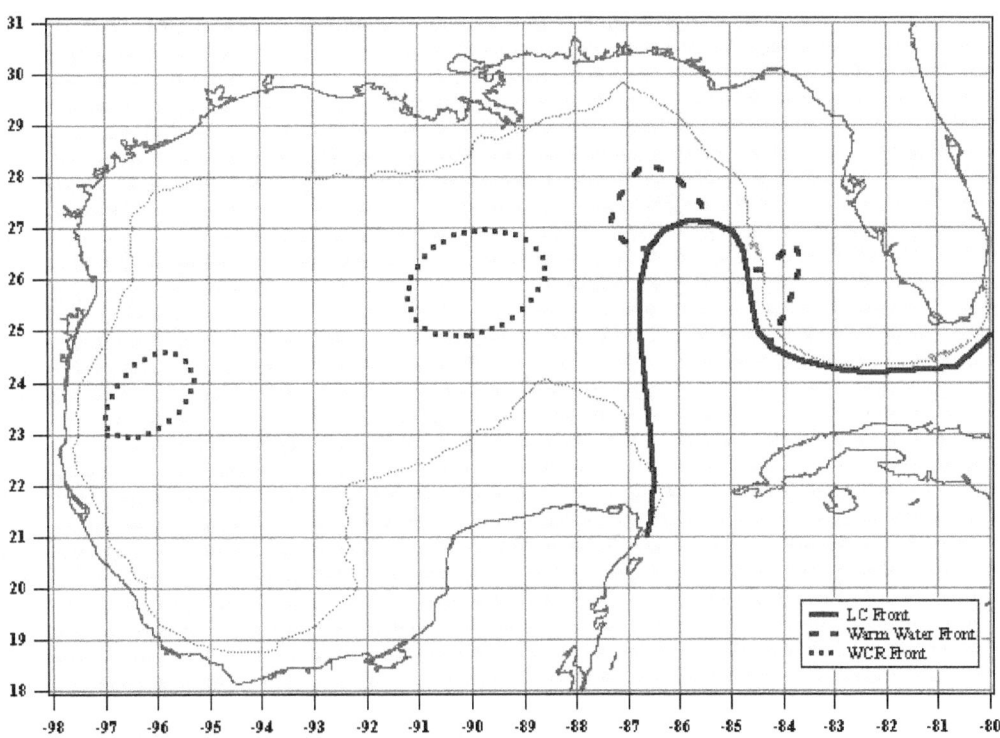

Figure 3.1. Example of an analysis of fronts in the GOM.

The solid blue line is the LC front and the dashed lines branching off of the LC are warm water features in the EGOM and on the WFS, the only source of the warm water being, of course, the LC. A more detailed discussion of the nature of these features will be given later in this report. The dotted lines represent the average position of the boundaries of WCRs in the WGOM.

11

The development of these front analyses is based, for the most part, on satellite remote sensing data (i.e., SST, ocean color, and sea-surface height [SSH] data from altimetry data). In the periods 1976 through 1978 and 1986 through 1991, only SST data were available to create the ocean front analysis in the GOM. Most of the SST data were obtained from the NOAA/AVHRR, though significant use was also made of GOES SST and SST data from NASA's Heat Capacity Mapping Mission (HCMM). As a result of using only SST data in the periods mentioned above, the frontal analyses could only be determined for as little as 5 months and as many as 8 months in a year, depending on when the mixed layer developed in the spring/summer and was removed in the autumn. However, in the periods when SST data were not useful, significant use was made of ship-of opportunity data to fill data gaps that existed in climatological data sets for certain ocean features in the GOM (e.g., position of the northern boundary of the LC, the location of WCRs centers, the month/year in which separation of a WCR from the LC occurred, etc). In the period 1979 through 1985, CZCS ocean color data were used to supplement the SST data, which were used to detect ocean features in the warm season when SST data were of little use. After 1991, TOPEX/ERS SSH data were available and the frontal analyses for most features could be developed for all twelve months in the year. After 1997, SeaWiFS and MODIS ocean color data were also used to supplement the SST data in the warm season to detect features that could not be detected in the SSH data (e.g., intrusions of LC water on the WFS).

4. THE LOOP CURRENT AND LOOP CURRENT WATER

4.1 Frequency of Loop Current Water in the EGOM

4.1.1. Introduction

The LC enters the EGOM through the Yucatan Strait and exits through the Straits of Florida (Maul et al., 1985). In the EGOM, the LC penetrates northward until instabilities form in the current and a WCR separates from the LC. As a result of this process, the amount of time that the water mass associated with the LC resides in any one location in the EGOM varies from one location to the next. The statistic presented in this section is the spatial frequency of water directly associated with the LC and provides information on the percent of time that the LC water mass resides at locations in the EGOM. This statistics can also be used to provide a crude estimate of the spatial frequency of the location of high speed current associated with the LC front in the EGOM. The statistic is based on a 28-year (i.e., 1976-2003) database, and was derived using, for the most part, satellite remote sensing data (i.e., IR SST, ocean color, and altimetry data).

4.1.2 Procedure

The frequency of LC water in the EGOM was determined using the LC frontal boundary analyses described in Section 3. A 0.5° latitude by 0.5° longitude grid was constructed and overlaid onto the frontal analyses. If the water mass associated with the LC occupied more than 50% of any 0.5° latitude by 0.5° longitude grid square in any given month, then it was assumed that the LC water mass was present in that grid square at that time. It should be noted that since this statistic was derived from monthly frontal analyses that depended primarily on satellite remote sensing data, there were periods (i.e., the mid 1970s and the late 1980s) when only SST data were available to create the LC frontal boundary analyses, and as a result, the LC front could only be determined for periods of 5 to 8 months in particular years, depending on when the mixed layer developed in the spring/summer and was removed in the autumn. When ocean color and/or altimetry data were available, the LC front was determined for all months in the year.

4.1.3 Analysis

Figure 4.1 presents the spatial frequency of the water mass associated with the LC in the EGOM. The LC frontal boundary seldom reached the 28° latitude line (i.e., about 5% of the time over the 28-year period). It reached the 27° latitude line about 20% of the time. *The LC usually penetrates about as far north as 27° N latitude just prior to WCR separation. After WCR separation, the LC re-establishes itself further south, usually at around 25° latitude, so that it does not normally occupy the northern part of the EGOM (i.e., north of 25 °N) for long periods of time.* The water mass associated with the LC occupied the region south of 24° N latitude and east of 86° W longitude the greatest amount of time. The analysis suggests that the LC was at times found on the Yucatan shelf and the West Florida Shelf. There are cases when LC thermal boundary that was determined using satellite SST imagery and ocean color imagery, were found at these locations. This, of course, does not mean that the high-speed currents associated with the LC were located on either shelf. The analysis shows that there is a mean westward tilt (i.e., a westward tilt of approximately 30°) of the axis of the frequency analysis. The variation of the orientation (i.e., the westward tilt) of the LC is associated with the separation of WCRs from the LC and will be discussed in detail in the next subsection.

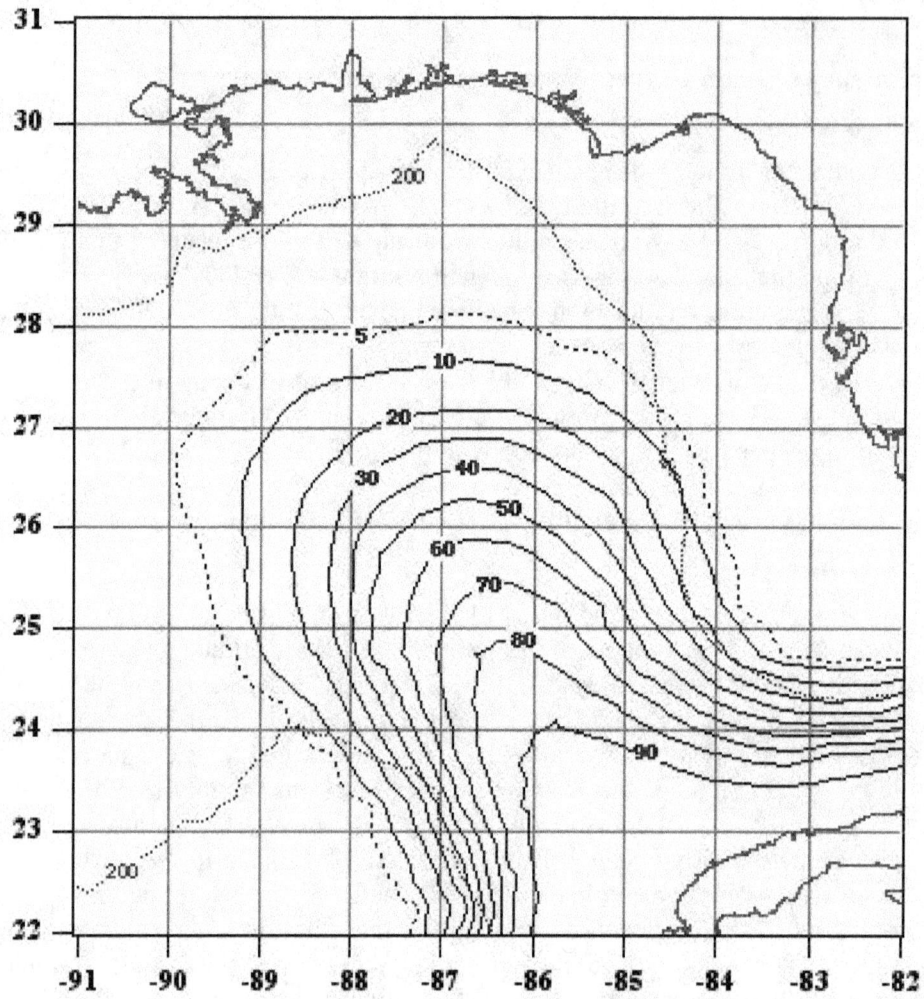

Figure 4.1. Spatial frequency (%) of the water mass associated with the LC in the EGOM based on data for the period 1976-2003

4.2 Orientation of the Loop Current

4.2.1 Introduction

The LC orientation is defined as the angle made by the intersection of a line drawn parallel to the eastern and western boundaries of the LC through the frontal axis and a longitude line. When a tilt of the axis of the LC occurs, it is always a westward tilt. *The orientation of the LC changes in association with cycle of the LC; that is, the northward penetration of the LC into the EGOM, the eventual separation of a WCR from the LC, and the re-establishment of the LC after eddy separation. The westward tilt of the LC is greatest at the time a WCR is about to separate. The orientation, or tilt, angle of the LC, is usually about 30°- 40°, on average, when a ring separates (i.e. the LC is oriented northwest-southeast).* However, much larger orientation angles (i.e., orientation angles the order of 60°) and tremendous westward extension of the LC have been observed in the last decade (Figure 4.2). When large tilt angles are achieved, the high-speed currents associated with the LC can influence central GOM and parts of the WGOM as Figure 4.2

14

indicates. *After the ring separates, the LC re-establishes itself around 25° N, in most cases, and, at that time, is oriented north-south (i.e., the orientation angle is 0°).* As the LC penetrates again into the EGOM, a westward tilt of the LC begins to emerge and the LC's orientation angle increases as processes associated with the LC lead once again to the separation of a WCR.

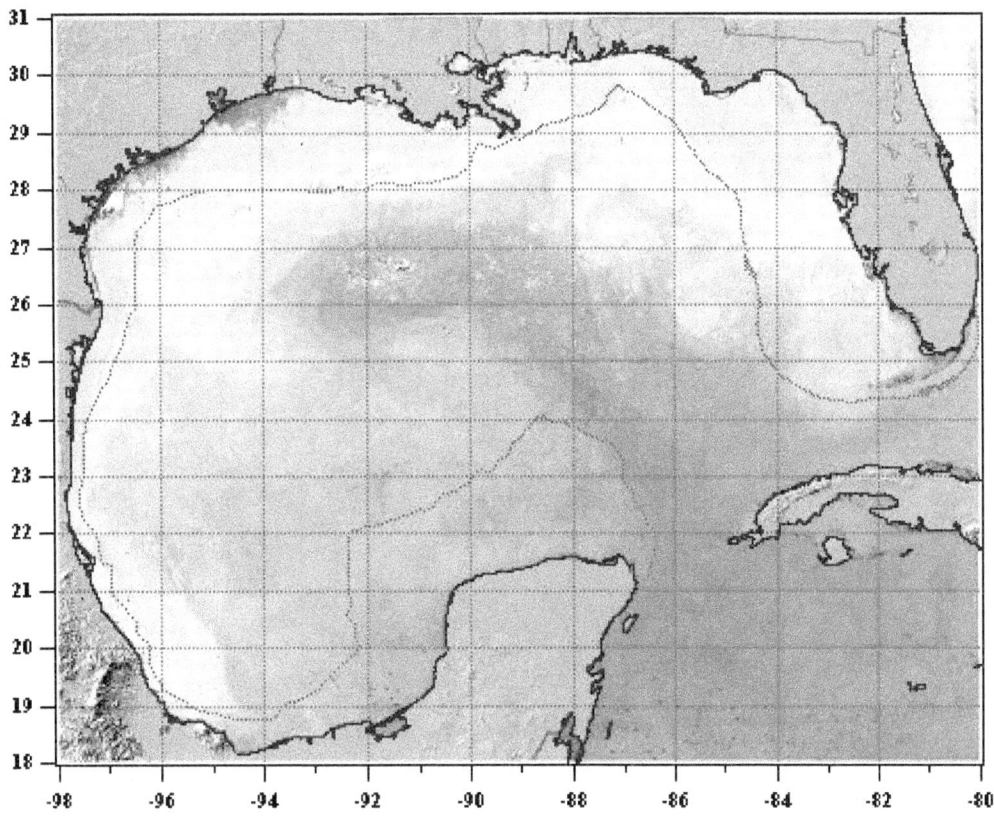

Figure 4.2. NOAA/AVHRR SST composite image for 31 January 2002. The LC orientation angle is on the order of 60° and the LC appears to extend as far west as 93° W in this case.

4.2.2 Procedure

The LC orientation was determined by drawing a straight line parallel to the eastern and western boundaries of the LC (Figure 4.3) and measuring the angle between that line and a longitude line (i.e., a line directed due north). These lines were drawn subjectively so that the angles determined are approximations. If that line was parallel to the longitude line, the orientation of the LC is north-south and the angle is zero degrees. If the line was parallel to a latitude line, the orientation of the LC is west-east and the angle is ninety degrees. The west-east LC orientation has never occurred in the more than 30 years that satellite data has been available to observe the LC behavior. As indicated previously, the maximum orientation angle observed to date was about 60°, which occurred in the last decade.

The LC orientation angle was determined for each month using the monthly frontal analyses. The data were used to determine standard statistics (i.e., the average, the mode, the standard deviation for the, the maximum, and the minimum orientation angle) and a frequency distribution for the orientation angle. The frequency distribution was established by binning the data in 5° increments (i.e., the binning took the form of 0°- 4°, 5°- 9°, 10°- 14°, etc.). The database for these statistics covered the period 1976-2003.

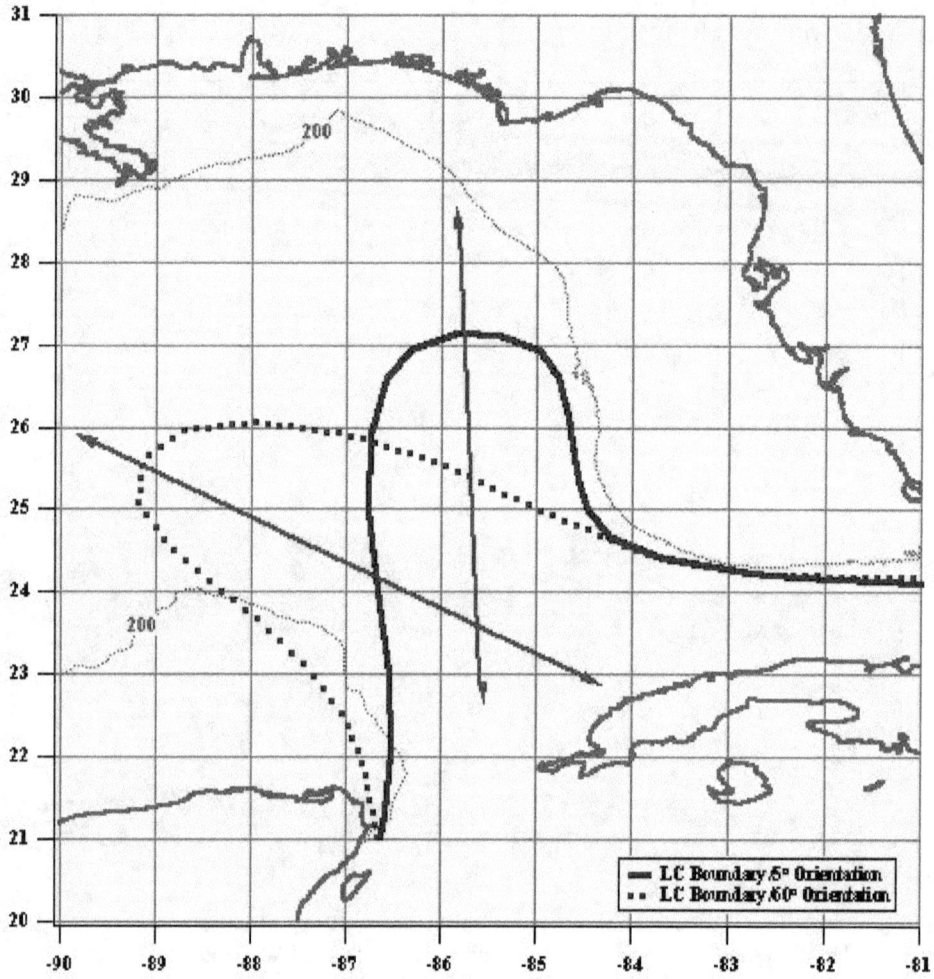

Figure 4.3. Depiction of method used to determine the Loop Current orientation angles.

As in the case of the frequency of LC water in the EGOM, this statistic was derived using monthly frontal analyses that depended primarily on satellite remote sensing data. As previously indicated, there were periods when only IR SST data were available to create the LC frontal boundary analyses, and as a result, the LC front could only be determined for 5 to 8 months in particular years, depending on when the mixed layer developed in the spring/summer and was removed in the autumn. When ocean color and/or altimetry data was available, the LC front was determined for all months in the year.

4.2.3 Analysis

Figure 4.4 provides the frequency distribution for the LC orientation angle. *The figure indicates that about 80% of the angles lie between 0° and 30° (i.e., the LC orientation is between north-south and north-north west--south-southeast). Orientation angles less than 30° are normally associated with a relatively stable LC (i.e., an LC not about to shed a WCR anytime in the near future). Orientation angles greater than 30° are found about 20% of the time. Normally when the LC orientation angles are this large, ring separation is soon to follow.* The primary mode in the histogram is in the 0°- 4° band. Secondary modes are noted in the bands 10°- 14° and 20°- 24°. These bands are orientation angles for a stable LC. The LC, at times, persists in these orientations for extended periods prior to separation process. Over the period 1976-2003, the average orientation angle was about 17° with a standard deviation of about 14°. The single most observed orientation angle (i.e., the mode of the data set) was 0°--a north-south orientation of the LC, which is, of course, the minimum angle observed. The maximum angle observed over the period was 63°. An angle greater than 55° only occurred twice over the 28-year period, and angles between 50°- 54° were also observed only twice.

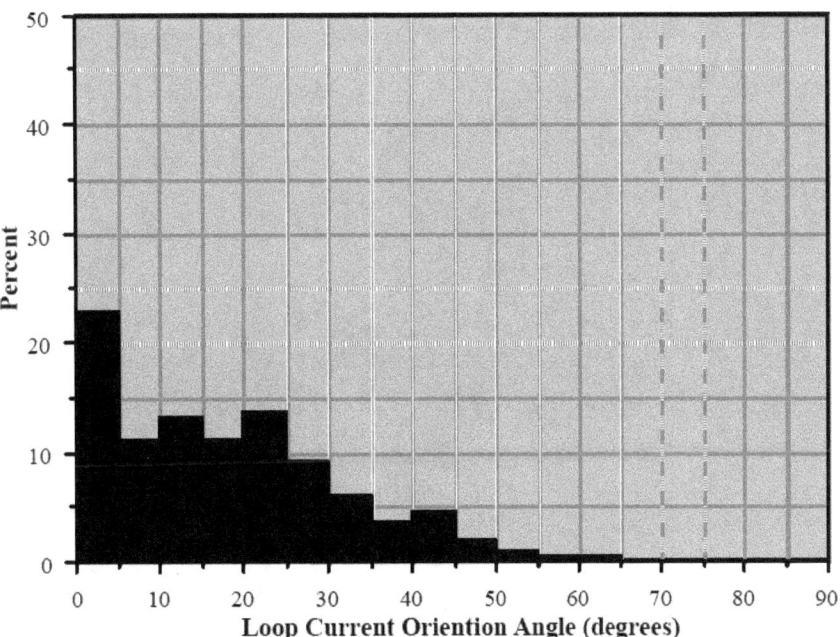

Figure 4.4 Frequency distribution for the Loop Current orientation angles. This analysis is based on data from the period 1976-2003.

4.3 Frequency of Isolated Warm Water in the EGOM

4.3.1 Introduction

Warm pools of water that become isolated from the LC, are often found in the EGOM. Though these warm water pools are isolated from the LC, the LC is the obvious source of these features. *They can be established in EGOM by minor, short-lived rings that separate from the LC and dissipate in the EGOM, by the advection of LC water by with the circulation associated with CCRs that are found on the northern boundary of the LC (Vukovich, 1988a; Wang et al., 2003), or by dragging surface water from the LC northward through the action of a strong wind stress. These pools are an indication of the transport of LC water mass and of any foreign mass (i.e., oil spilled, dinoflagellates, etc.) residing in the LC, from the LC into the common water area of the EGOM.* Figure 4.5 is a NOAA/AVHRR SST image showing various types of warm pools that can be found in the EGOM. The warm pool north and somewhat west of the LC may be the result of a small WCR separating from the LC or it may be due to northward advection of LC water by the CCR that is located at the northwestern boundary of the LC. The warm water pool that is located near the eastern boundary of the LC, and which is partially on the WFS, is due to transport of LC water by the CCR that is found along the LC's eastern boundary. The analysis that was created and described in this section provides specific information on the spatial frequency of these warm pools and in so doing, gives an indication of the frequency of processes that create the pools.

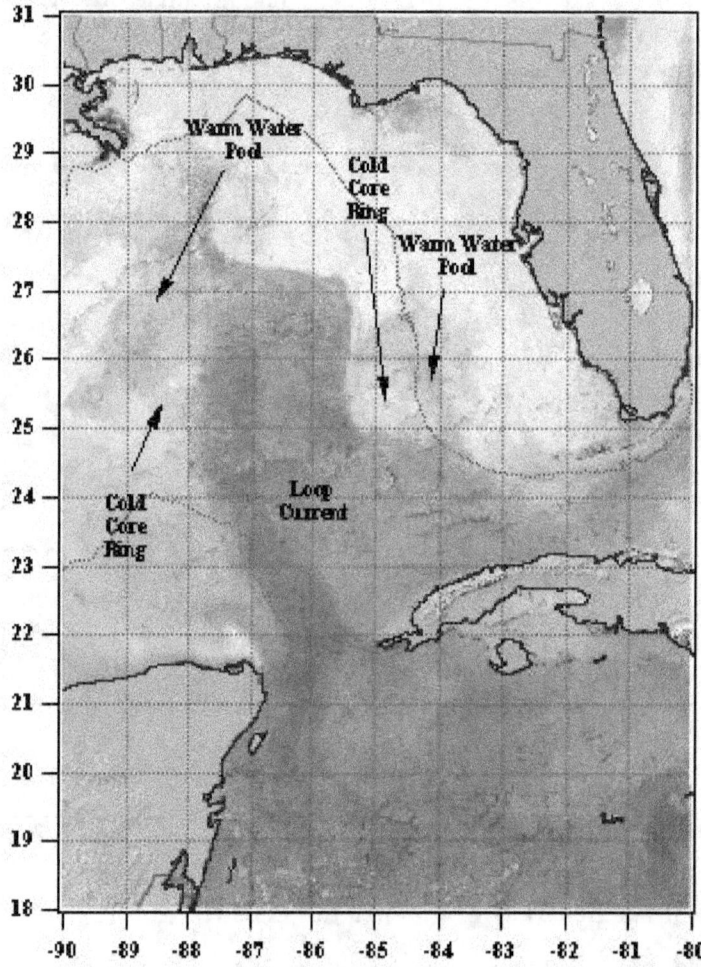

Figure 4.5. NOAA/AVJRR SST image for 16 February 1999 depicting warm water pools in the EGOM.

4.3.2 Procedure

To produce the analysis of the spatial distribution of the frequency of the isolated warm pools water in the EGOM, a 0.5° latitude by 0.5° longitude grid, identical to the one used to obtain the spatial frequency of LC water, was used in the EGOM. The frequency was determined for each grid square by overlaying the grid on the characteristic monthly ocean frontal analyses. For each grid square, the number of times that an isolated warm water pool encompassed that grid-point, was determined over the database period. As in the case of the spatial frequency of the LC, if the water mass associated with a warm pool occupied more than 50% of a grid square in any given month, then it was assumed that the water mass was present in that grid square at that time. It should be noted that these features could only be detected using satellite ocean color and SST data, and therefore, suffer from the lack of data in the warm seasons when only SST data were available. When ocean color data were available, these features could be determined for all months in the year. This analysis used data for a 28-year period (1976-2003).

4.3.3 Analysis

Figure 4.6 provides the spatial frequency of the isolated warm water pools in the EGOM. Pools of LC water were found throughout the region north of 25° N in the EGOM over the period. The highest frequency, at which those pools were found, was approximately 14 percent and the center of high frequency was located immediately west of the shelf break of the WFS at about 27.25 °N and 85.25 °W. *This high frequency feature was created, for the most part, as a result of many cases in which there was advection of warm LC water by the circulation associated with CCRs, which were located on the northeastern boundary of the LC (See the example in Figure 4.7).* The 14 percent maximum frequency corresponds to a frequency of about 1 event every 10 months or about 7 events in 6 years.

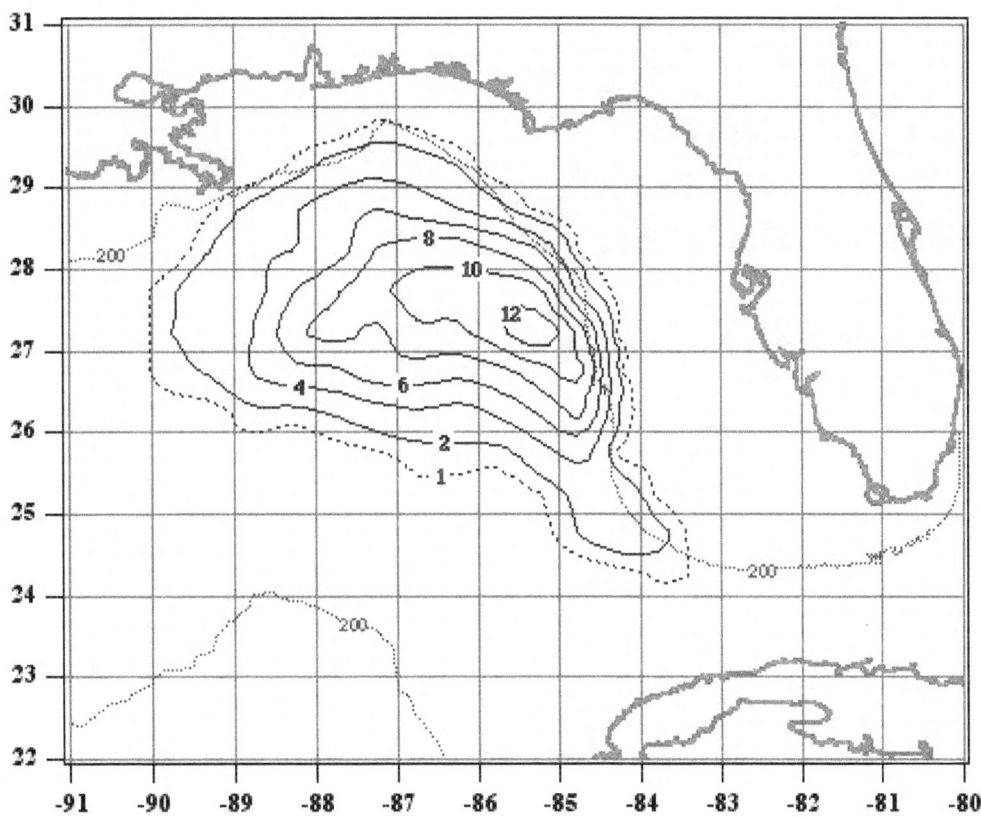

Figure 4.6. Spatial frequency (%) of isolated warm pools in the EGOM based on data for the period 1976-2003.

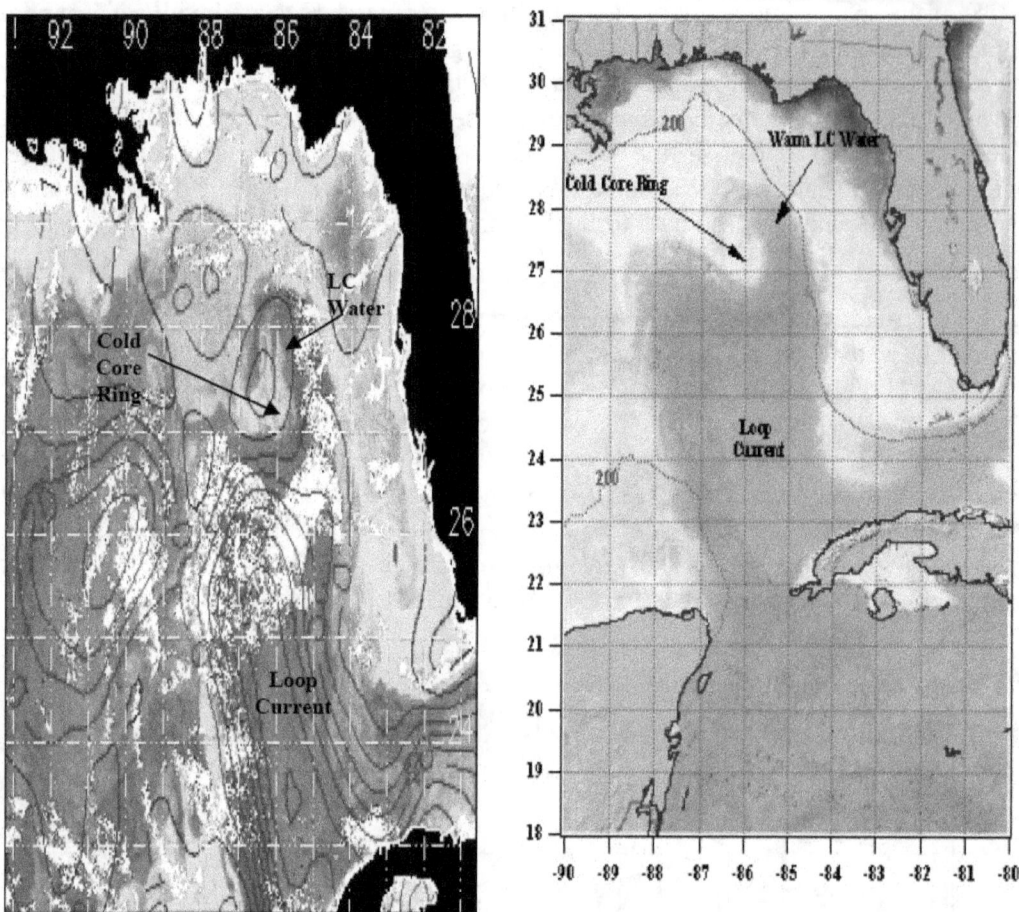

Figure 4.7. SeaWiFS ocean color image for 18 January 2000 with TOPEX altimetry data superimposed (left figure); NOAA/AVHRR SST image for 23 January 2000. Both data sets show the northward transport of LC water by a CCR in the northeast part of the LC (right figure).

There is also an interesting feature in the analysis that is located at around 29° N and 87.25 'W. This feature is described in the 4 percent isoline where it extends northward toward the DeSoto Canyon area. That feature was principally a result of minor, short-lived rings, which moved northward into the DeSoto Canyon area and then dissipated. Warm water advection associated with CCR also played a role in creating this feature, but this process played a minor role. In the spring 1977, significant amounts of surface water from the Loop Current were transported northward into the DeSoto Canyon area solely by the effect of a strong wind stress, which also contributed to this frequency feature. The highest frequency in this region that suggests an extension into DeSoto Canyon was about 5 percent. A 5-percent frequency corresponds to about 1 event every 2.5 years.

It should be noted that the association of a frequency value with an event, which is directly related to a process, in this case and cases discussed later in this report, does not necessarily refer to separate events. This is particularly true in those cases when a frequency value is associated with more than one event per year. An event may persist for more than a month in a given location, creating a frequency that is related to the event's persistence rather than to multiple occurrences of similar events in that case.

4.4 Frequency of Loop Current Water on the West Florida Shelf

4.4.1 Introduction

The cyclonic circulation associated with CCRs on the eastern boundary of the LC occasionally cause a transport of warm LC water onto the WFS (See the example in Figure 4.8). In time, the LC water mass mixes with the shelf water, so that the LC water mass is no longer distinguishable from shelf water using satellite SST or ocean color data. As in the previous case, *the transport of LC water onto the shelf also means that any foreign mass (i.e., oil spilled, dinoflagellates, etc.) residing in the LC will also be transported onto the shelf.* This analysis provides specific information on the spatial frequency of warm LC water that was transported onto the WFS and in so doing, provides information on the frequency of processes that cause this kind of transport.

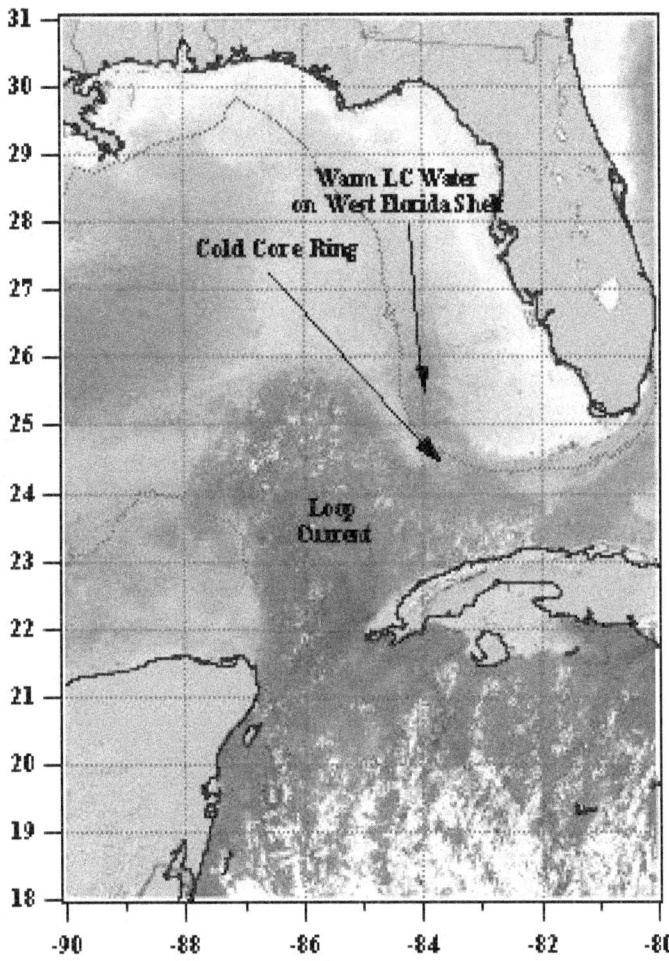

Figure 4.8. NOAA/AVHRR SST image for 15 November 1999.

4.4.2 Procedure

The procedure to obtain the spatial frequency of LC water on the WFS is similar to that for the spatial frequency of the LC in the EGOM and the spatial frequency of isolated warm water pools in the EGOM. A 0.5° latitude by 0.5° longitude grid was constructed

21

and overlaid onto the frontal analyses, which indicated the presence of LC water on the WFS. For each grid square, the number of times that LC water was found in that grid square was determined over the database period. As in previous cases, if the warm water mass on the shelf occupied more than 50% of a grid square in any given month, then it was assumed that the water mass was present in that grid square at that time. It should be noted that this feature could only be detected using satellite ocean color and SST data. Therefore, this analysis suffered from the applicability of SST data in the warm season in periods when only SST data were available. The database used for this analysis covered the period 1976-2003.

4.4.3 Analysis

The analysis of the spatial frequency of warm LC water on the WFS shows that intrusions of LC water onto the shelf occurred most often south of 27° N and between the (i.e., the 200-m isobath) and the 83° W longitude line (Figure 4.9); that is, most of these intrusions occurred near the shelf break and do not penetrate deep into the shelf (i.e., they do not penetrate deep into the shelf as an identifiable features in the satellite remote sensing data). The apparent lack of identifiable deep penetration of these features on the shelf is presumably due to mixing. *It also appears that the intrusions of LC water onto the shelf occurs most often when a CCR, whose circulation causes the transport, is located on the southeastern portion of the LC front near the Dry Tortugas.* The maximum spatial frequency for these events is about 12%, which correspond to a frequency of about 1 event every year, in this case.

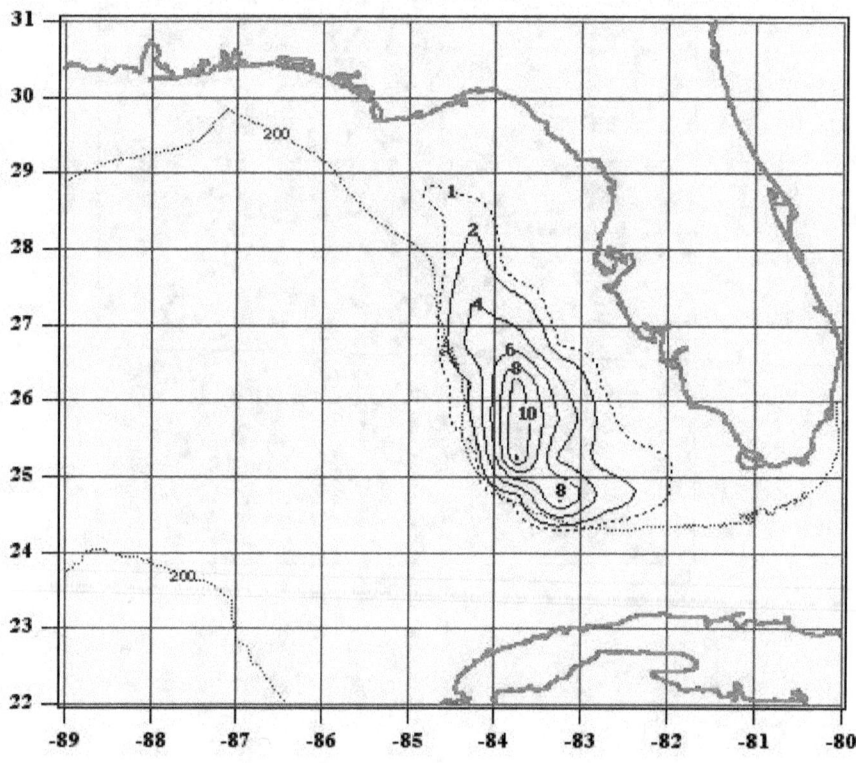

Figure 4.9. Spatial frequency (%) of LC water on the West Florida shelf based on data for the period 1976-2003.

It should be noted that the circulation on the WFS can possibly augment or deter the effects of the intrusions of LC water onto the shelf. A program sponsored by the MMS examined the circulation on the WFS in 1996. The shelf was seeded with hundreds of satellite-tracked surface drifters during that year. The drifter data was used to determine the characteristic circulation on the shelf by integrating all drifter locations for the a given month in that year and using those data to determine the speed and direction of the flow at the surface on the shelf for that month. Figure 4.10 shows the surface flow on the WFS for the months of March, August, and November 1996. Super-imposed on the figure are satellite SST data (i.e., color coded) and SSH contours from satellite altimetry data. The analyses in Figure 4.10 show flow to the south-southeast on the WFS in March and November 1996 and flow to north-northwest in August 1996.

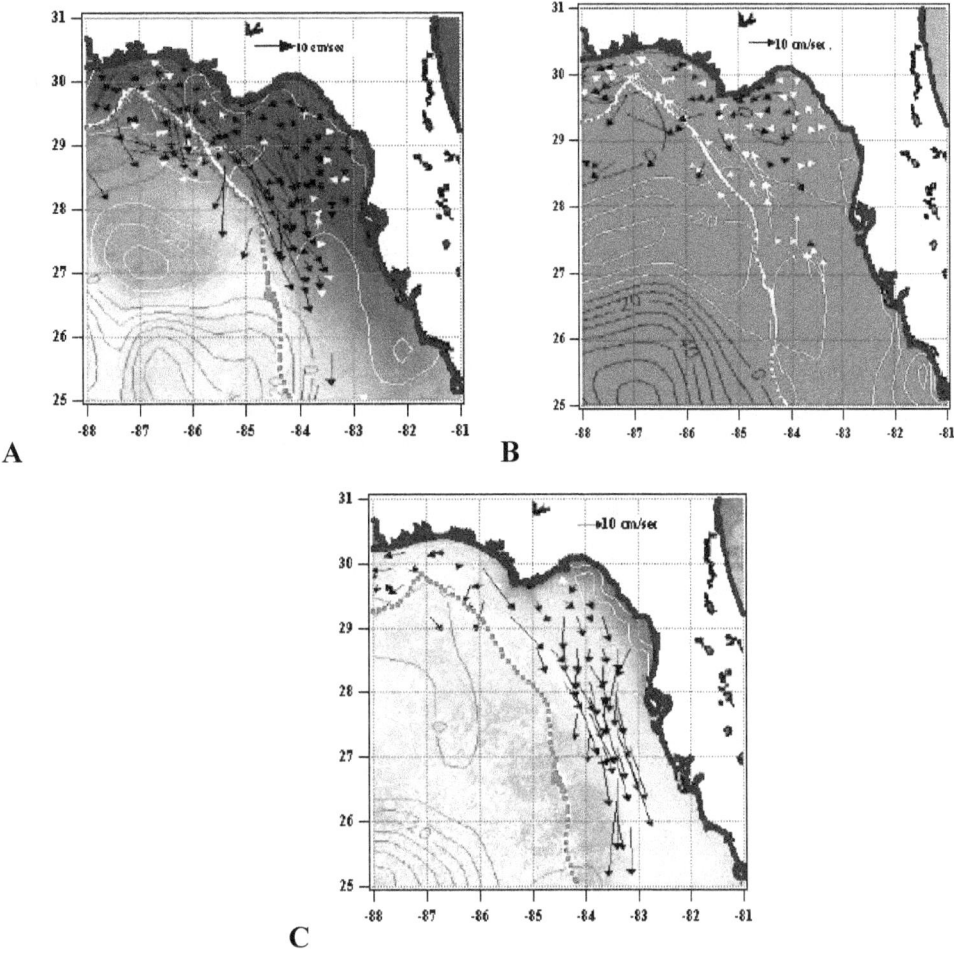

Figure 4.10. Surface currents on the West Florida Shelf from surface drifter data for (A) March 1996, (B) August 1996, and (C) November 1996. Super-imposed are satellite SST and SSH data.

Figure 4.11 provides the mean monthly current speed and direction at 28° N and 84° W that were derived from the drifter data. *The data in that figure shows that southerly currents, which would prevent the widespread northward transport of LC water and any mass in the intruded water mass on the shelf, were found on the shelf in the fall and winter. Northerly currents, which would augment widespread northward transport of LC water on the shelf, were noted in the spring and summer.* Data were not available to determine whether the 1996 data represent the characteristic cycle of the surface flow on that shelf each year. However, it should be noted that the shelf currents are controlled by the wind (He and Weisberg, 2003), and they will vary as the year-to-year wind climatology varies.

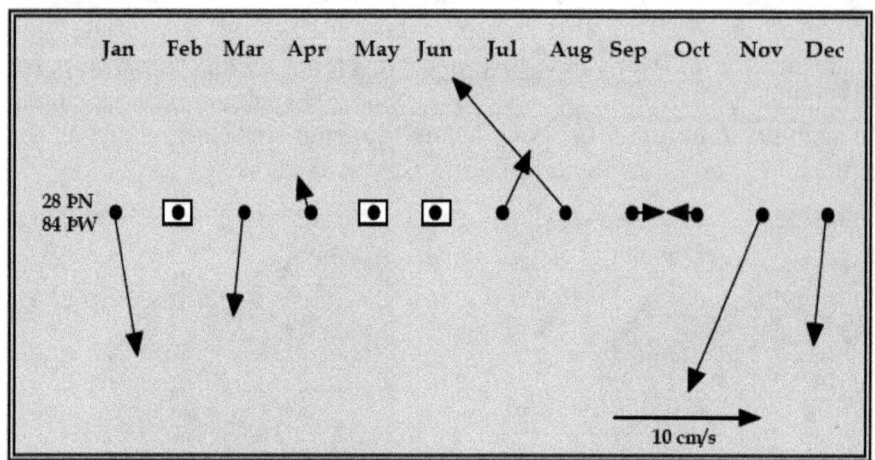

Figure 4.11. Monthly mean sea-surface velocity vectors on the WFS (28 °N, 84 °W) from surface drifter data for 1996. An open square around the black dot means no data were available at the location. North is toward the top of the page.

5. WARM CORE RINGS

5.1 Frequency of Ring Separation

5.1.1 Introduction

A considerable number of studies have appeared in the peer-reviewed literature, which focused on the separation frequency of large WCRs from the LC. The separation periods that have been reported are highly variable: 8-9 months (Vukovich and Maul, 1985); 11 months (Vukovich, 1988a; Maul and Vukovich, 1993; Vukovich, 1995); 12 months (Sturges and Evans, 1983); bimodal periods of 8-9 months and 13-14 months (Sturges, 1992, 1994); and bimodal periods 6 and 11 months with a minor mode at 9 months (Sturges and Leben, 2000). *Sturges and Leben (2000) also noted that with considerable smoothing of the spectrum, the peak distribution was formed around 12-month periods. Vukovich (1988a, 1995) and Maul and Vukovich (1993) noted that the 11-month period that they cited is an average value and that the eddy separation periods were highly variable, ranging from 6-17 months. The eddy-shedding period seldom was the same as the average period or any of the other characteristic values cited in the literature.*

The studies cited above used data sets with periods as small as 10 years and as large as 26 years. The variable nature of the results from these studies is, in part, a testimonial to the limitations in deriving statistics using data sets that are small when the statistic deals with events that occur a very limited number of times in a year. Vukovich (1995) suggested that it may be necessary to require data sets that cover a 100-year period in order the obtain a statistically stable estimate of the eddy-shedding period. In this section of this report, the eddy-shedding period was re-examined using the largest data set currently available (i.e., a 32-year data set). The period was actually examined using two procedures: a histogram of eddy-shedding periods using a 32-year data set and spectral analysis of the LC northern boundary oscillations using a 27-year data set.

5.1.2 Procedure

The eddy-shedding period was examined using two procedures. In one procedure, a histogram of the eddy-separation periods was developed. The eddy-separation periods were determined by documenting the month and year of the separation of each major ring. A major ring was defined as a large ring (i.e., rings with diameters of about 300 km or more at the time that they separated from the LC.), which persisted for more than five months. The month and year of separation was that time when the major eddy completely separated from the LC. In some cases, a WCR separated from the LC only to be re-absorbed by the LC. In some cases, a WCR separated from the LC twice only to be re-absorbed by the LC. The month and year of separation of the ring from the LC for this study was defined as the month and year when complete separation occurred and the ring moved into the WGOM. Furthermore, this study only dealt with rings that actually separated from the LC. There are situations when large rings develop near the LC (Figure 5.1) for no apparent reason. As the figure shows, a large ring developed immediately west of the LC and another ring that was centered at about 23.3 N and 93.7 W on 15 June, intensified in about 25 days. There are indications in the 1 July analysis that an energy pulse may have emanated from the LC. In any case, there was obviously no separation of a WCR from the LC in this case and the ring that developed was not considered in this analysis.

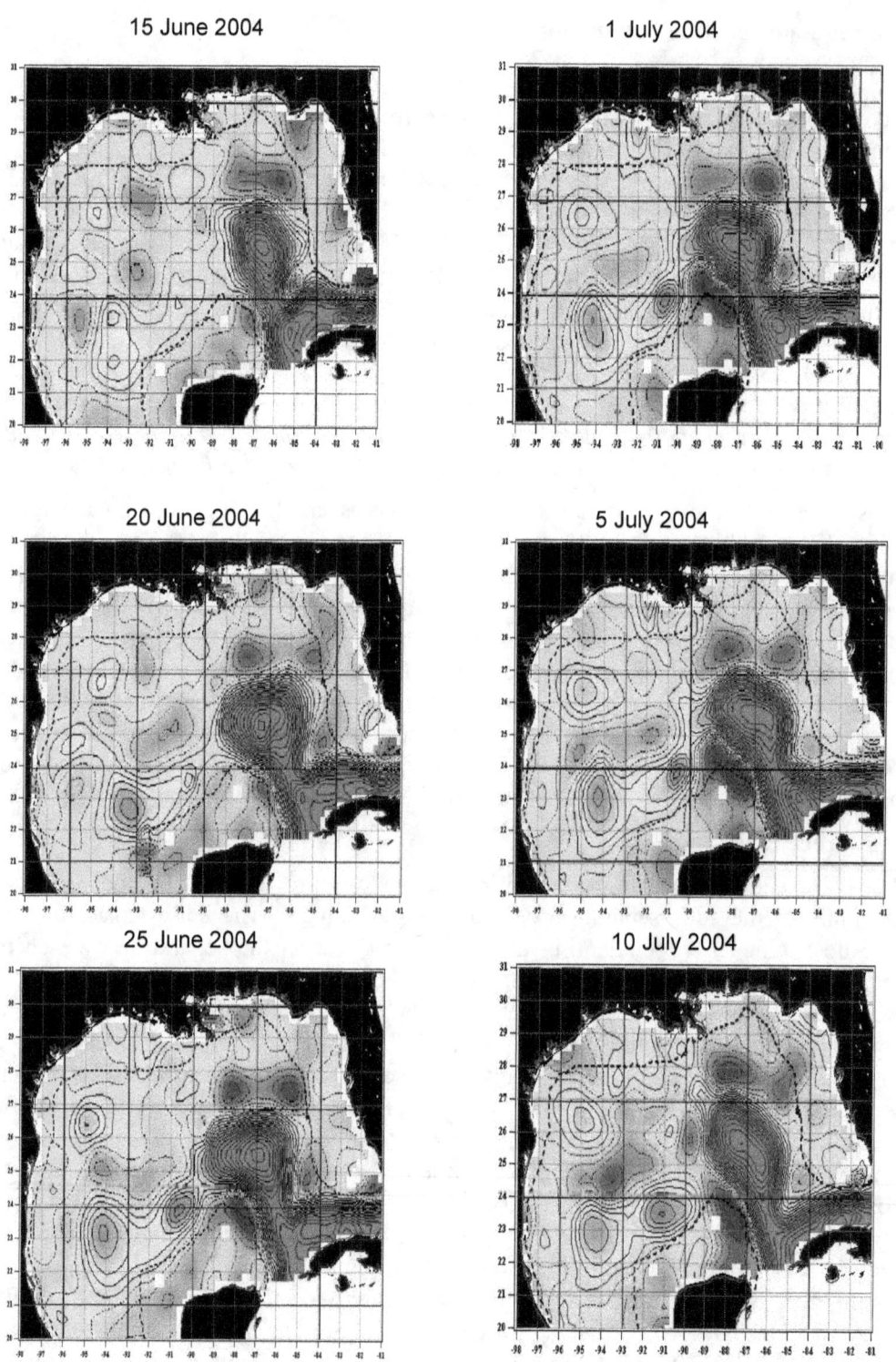

Figure 5.1. Time series of SSH analyses from TOPEX/Poseiden showing the apparent development of a WRC immediately west and slightly south of the LC.

A 32-year (i.e., 1972-2003) data set was used to determine the eddy-separation periods, and in that period, 37 major rings separated from the LC. Under normal circumstances, one major WCR separated from the LC each year. In some years, two rings separated, but these usually separated in different months as little as 5 months apart. In 2002 however, two major rings separated from the LC in the same month (Figure 5.2). Two rings also separated from the LC in the same month in 2003, but one of these dissipated quickly (i.e., in about three months), so that it was not considered to be a major ring.

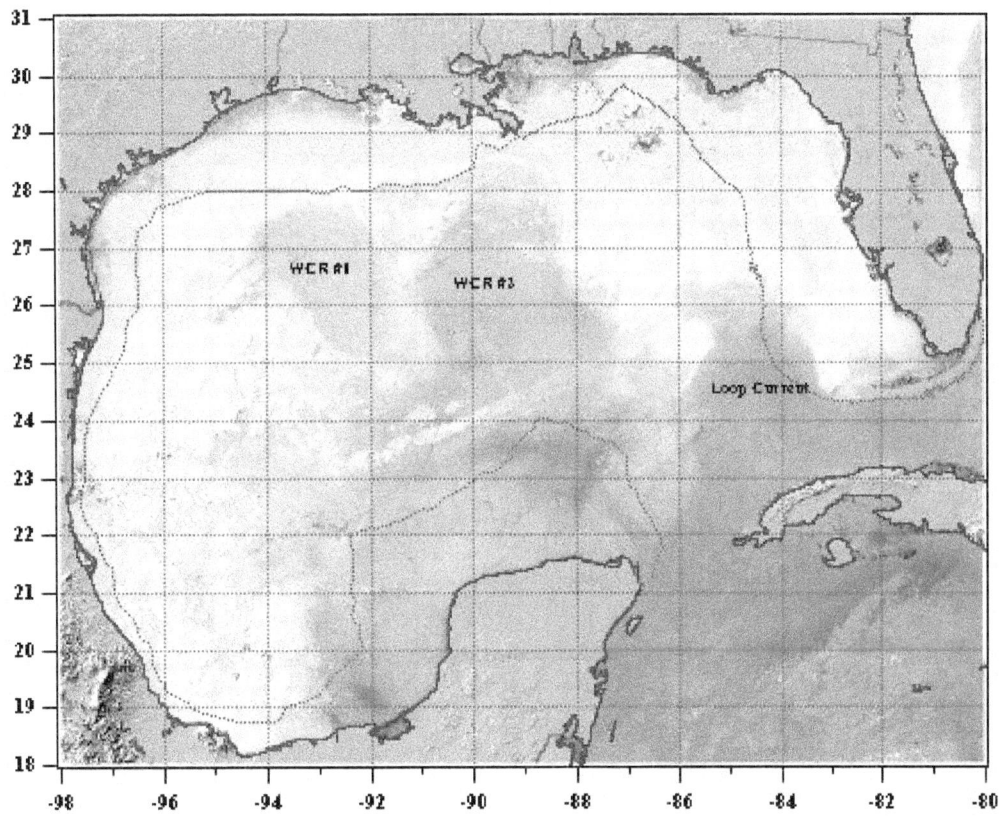

Figure 5.2. NOAA/AVHRR SST image for 15 March 2002 shows two WCRs that separated from the LC in March 2002. The dual separation was the result of the elongated LC noted in Figure 4.2 in Section 4.

For the second approach, a time series of the mean monthly distances between the northern most boundary of the LC and the 30° N latitude line (Figure 5.3) was developed using the frontal analyses discussed previously. The average distance for a given year was calculated using the monthly averaged values and was subtracted from each corresponding monthly averaged value to produce detrended, monthly displacements of the northern boundary relative to the mean. A sign convention was developed such that positive displacements were to the north of the mean (Figure 5.4). Spectral analysis was applied to the time series of detrended, monthly displacements of the northern boundary to determine dominant periods. *It should be noted that when the LC penetrates into the EGOM, the northern boundary generally moves north of its mean annual position. When a major eddy separates from the LC, the northern boundary moves abruptly south of its mean annual position because the eddy is no longer considered as part of the LC (Figure*

27

5.5). As a result, the LC's northern boundary moves north and south of its mean annual position with a frequency, which is, for the most part, associated with eddy shedding. Therefore, the dominant periods from the spectral analysis of these displacements will provide an indication of the dominant eddy-shedding period. A 27-year (i.e., 1977-2003) data set was used to study the LC northern boundary oscillations.

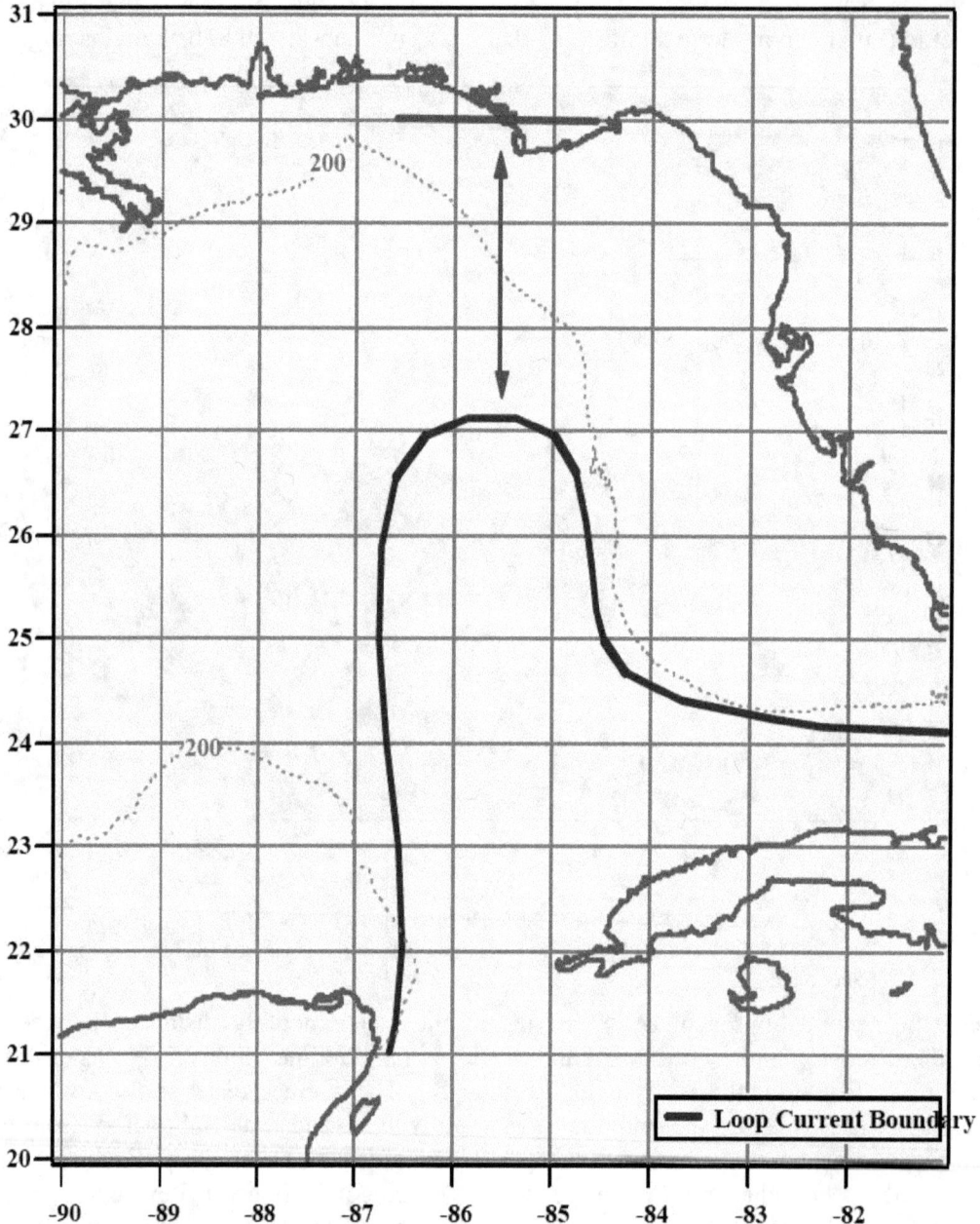

Figure 5.3. Measurement procedure for the Loop Current's northern boundary.

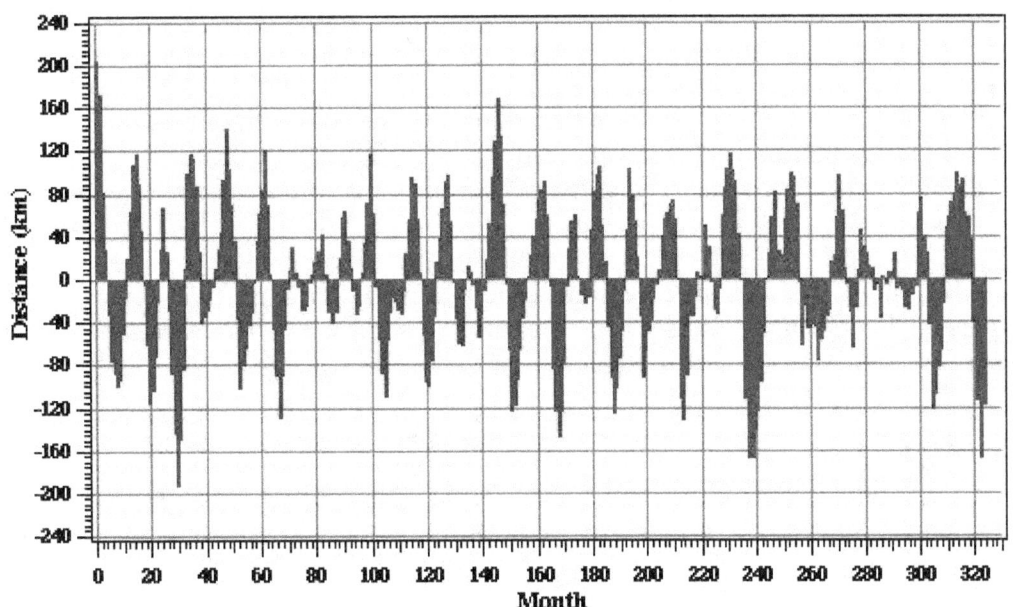

Figure 5.4. LC's northern boundary displacements in the period 1977-2003.

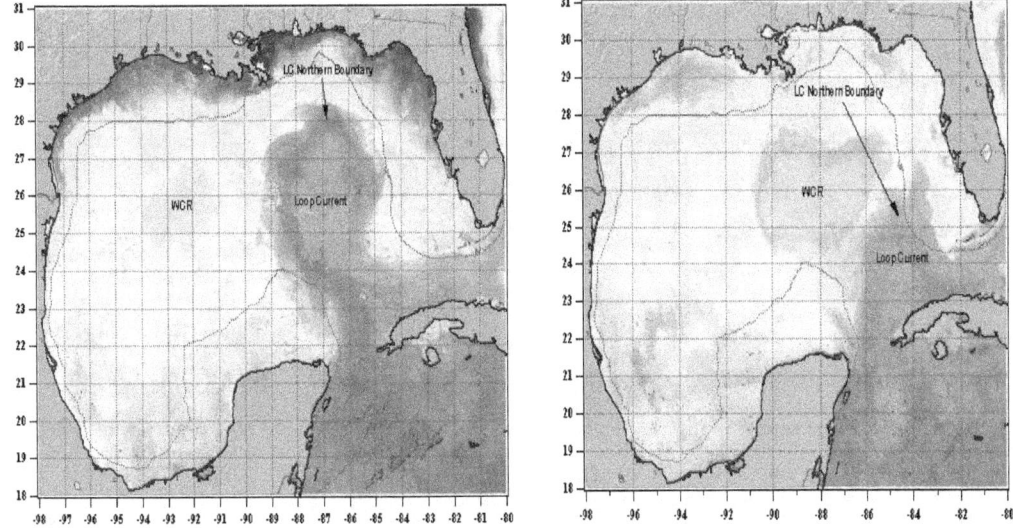

Figure 5.5. NOAA/AVHRR SST images for the period February-March 1998 depicting a ring separation event. The image on the left is for 6 February 1998 and that on the right is for 30 march 1998. The images show the rapid shift of the position of the LC's northern boundary from about 28° N in early February to about 26° N in late March.

The spectrum of the LC northern boundary variations was calculated using a spectral analysis routine, which was part of the IGOR Pro software package. One Hanning smoothing of the spectrum was applied.

5.1.3 Analysis

Figure 5.6 provides a histogram of the LC's eddy-shedding periods for the period 1972-2003. The frequency distribution is bimodal with primary modes at 6 and 11 months, similar to that found by Sturges and Leben (2000). The primary modes have frequencies of 14%. The range in the data is 5 to 19 months, and the average eddy-shedding period is 11 months with a standard deviation of ± 4 months. Since the average period and one of the primary modes in the histogram are approximately 11 months, this might suggest that an 11-month period is a representative period for eddy separation from the LC. However, since periods of 6, 9, 10, and 14 months also have significant frequencies, *it is more likely that the eddy-shedding period is highly variable and that no one period can be used to represent the LC's eddy-shedding period.* Oey et al. (2003) has suggested that the variability of the LC eddy-shedding frequency is a function of three factors: a) the steadiness of the transport; b) wind-induced fluctuations through the Greater Antilles Passage; and c) Caribbean eddies. Their results suggest that any one of these factors can induce a shorter or longer eddy-shedding period.

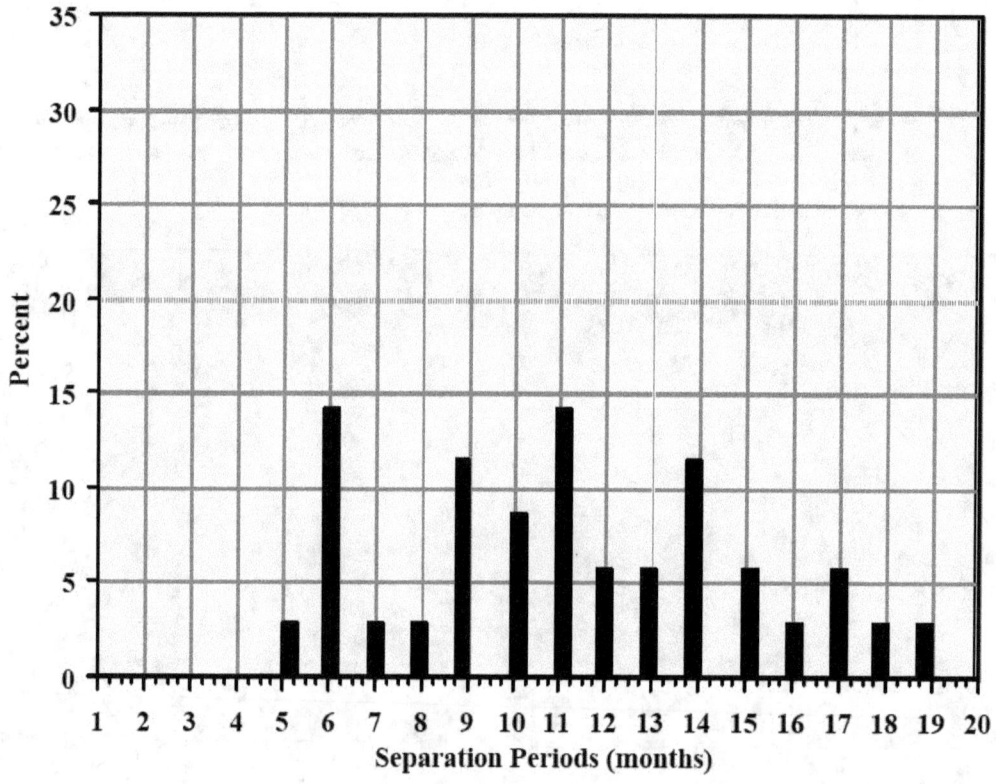

Figure 5.6. Histogram of the LC's eddy-shedding periods for the period 1972-2003.

Figure 5.7 provides the histogram for the LC's eddy shedding as a function of the month in the year. *The mode of the frequency distribution is at month 3 (March) and the average is month 6 (June). The standard deviation is ± 3 months. These data indicated that about 45% of the major WCRs separated from the LC in the late winter and spring period (i.e., March, April, May, and June). It is interesting to note that over the 32-year period, no WCRs separated from the LC in month 12 (i.e., December) and the net frequency for eddy shedding is a minimum in months 11 and 12 (i.e., November-December). This is the same period when the Straits of Florida transport is normally a minimum (Maul and Vukovich, 1993).*

30

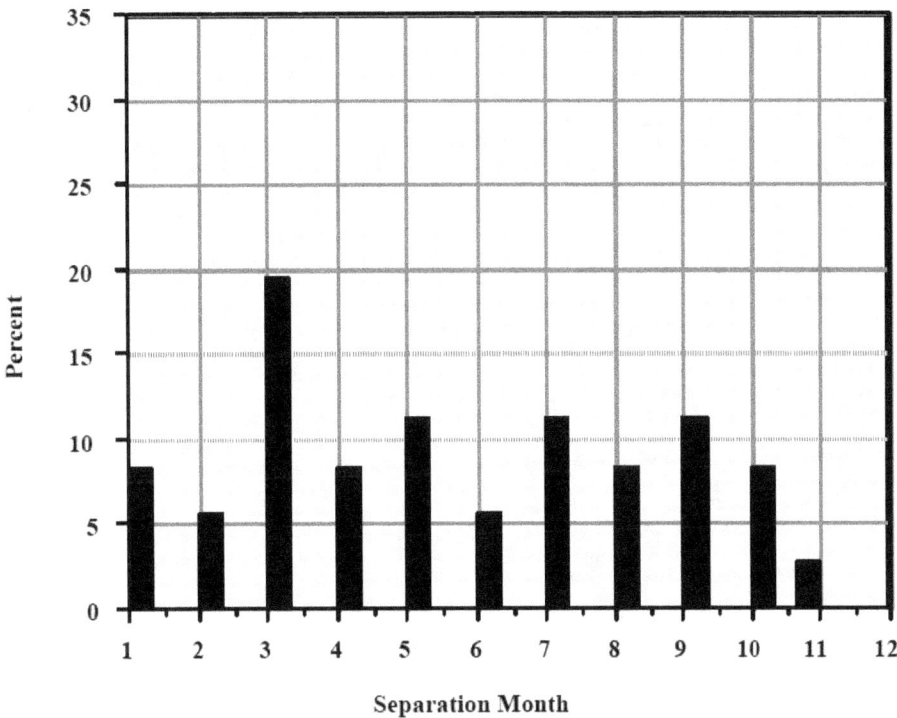

Figure 5.7. Histogram of the LC eddy separation as a function of month in a year based on data for the period 1972-2003.

Figure 5.8 provides the variance-preserved spectrum of the data in Figure 5.4. A one-time Hanning filter has been applied to the spectrum. The most significant variance has a period of 12.0 months, which is one month larger than one of the modes in the histogram (Figure 5.5) and the average of the eddy-shedding periods from the data used in the histogram procedure. There are secondary peaks in the spectrum at 9.5 months and 8.1 months. The histogram (Figure 5.6) has a secondary mode at 9 months. *It should be noted that the period having the most significant variance in the spectrum varied by one month over the last 10 years as each additional year of data was add to the data set of LC's northern boundary displacements data (Table 5.1); that is, it varied from 12.2 months to 11.1 months and then back to 12 months over the 10-year period, which is most probably a consequence of the fact that the eddy-shedding period was highly variable over that period. On the other hand, the average eddy-shedding period that was derived using the data set that was used to create histograms (Figure 5.6) remained about 11 months over the past 10 years (Table 5.1) as the eddy-shedding periods that took place each year were added to the data set, suggesting that the average eddy-shedding statistic may be a stable statistic.*

5.2 Ring Path

5.2.1 Introduction

When major WCRs separate from the LC, they move into the WGOM. Their direction of motion is generally westward until they reach the "western wall" of the GOM (Vukovich

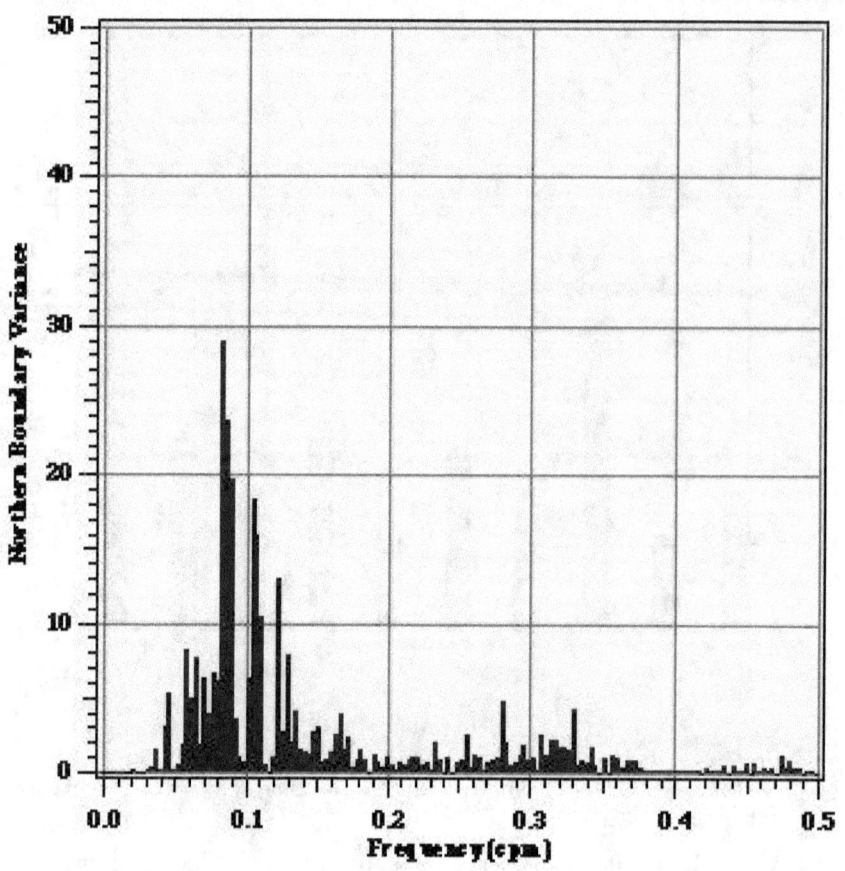

Figure 5.8. Variance-preserved spectrum of the LC's northern boundary variations based on data for the period 1977-2003

Table 5.1. Year-to-Year Change in the Period Having the Most Significant Variance from the Spectrum and in the Average Eddy-Shedding Period from the Histogram Data Set over the Last Decade

Year	Period Having the Most Significant Variance from Spectrum (months)	Average Eddy-Shedding Period from the Histogram Data Set (months)
1994	12.2	11.3
1995	12.2	10.8
1996	12.2	10.9
1997	12.1	11.0
1998	12.2	10.8
1999	11.5	11.1
2000	11.5	11.1
2001	11.5	11.3
2002	11.1	11.3
2003	12.0	11.3

and Waddell, 1991; Elliott, 1982; Hamilton et al., 1999). During their movement from the EGOM through the WGOM, *some rings have their centers located north of 26° N most of the time*. Since these major WCR are large (i.e., having diameters of about 300-400 km), *the circulation associated with these rings under these circumstances interact with the Louisiana and Texas shelf and the slope region west of 90° W. Many rings have their centers located between 24° N and 26° N when they move through the WGOM*. These rings travel through the deep Gulf regions (i.e., water depths ≥ 2000 m) for the most part, but most of *the very large WCRs will affect the slope region west of 90° W, especially when their path is in the northern part of the 24° N - 26° N latitude belt*. Some rings move southwestward from the EGOM into the WGOM (i.e., move into the region south of 24° N), then turn northward as they approach the western wall. Sutyrin et al. (2003) has suggested that the westward motion of rings is governed by the presence or absence of a deep circulation associated with the ring and the configuration of the northwest corner of the shelf. *After reaching the western wall, the WCRs generally have no prescribed direction of motion. Some rings move northward. Some move southward, while others move eastward*. In this section of this report, the frequency at which major WRCs move along three paths through the WGOM to the western wall is determined using data for the period 28-year period 1976-2003.

5.2.2 Procedure

For each month in the period 1976-2003, the mean positions of the centers of the major WCRs were determined. The center of these rings was determined in most cases as the geometric center. When altimetry data were available, the center of the ring was defined as the location of the largest value for the sea-surface height. Major rings that coalesced with other rings and rings that the split, producing two rings, during their motion through the WGOM were excluded from this analysis. The mean monthly ring positions were plotted (Figure 5.9) in the WGOM. It should be noted that only major rings were included in the analysis (i.e., minor rings were excluded) and only their path from the EGOM to the western wall was considered (i.e., their path after reaching the western wall was not included in this analysis). Those rings that spent 75% or more of the time north of 26° N before reaching the western wall were considered to have the Northern Path. Those that spent 75% or more of the time between 24° N and 26° N were considered to have the Central Path, and those that spent 75% or more of the time south of 24° were considered to have the Southern Path. The database used for this study included satellite remote sensing data (i.e., IR SST data, ocean color data, and altimetry data), analyzed in-situ data from ships of opportunity and from MMS field programs in the GOM, information from the GOM programs managed by the various oil and gas companies, and satellite-track drifter data. The drifter data was especially useful in the summer periods when ocean color and/or altimetry data were not available.

5.2.3 Analysis

Figure 5.10 provided the frequency analysis for the three ring paths examined. *By far, the preferred path (i.e., with a frequency of 62%) for the WCRs through the WGOM is the Central Path*. As indicated previously, the WCRs that travel along the Central Path, move through the deep-water regions of the WGOM. However, if the WCR is especially large and if it moves through the north portions of the latitude belt that defines the Central Path (i.e., 24° N –26° N), the circulation associated with these rings will influence the slope region off the Texas-Louisiana coast west of 90° W. *The Northern Path, which is the WCR path that will allow the rings to influence the Louisiana and Texas shelf and the slope west of 90° W, has the next highest frequency (i.e., 24%). The least likely path for the WCRs is the Southern Path with a frequency of about 14%.* It should be noted that Hamilton et al. (1999) found no apparent preferred path for the WCRs. They examined 10 WCRs between 1985 and 1995. Their findings were based on a significantly smaller dataset than used in this study.

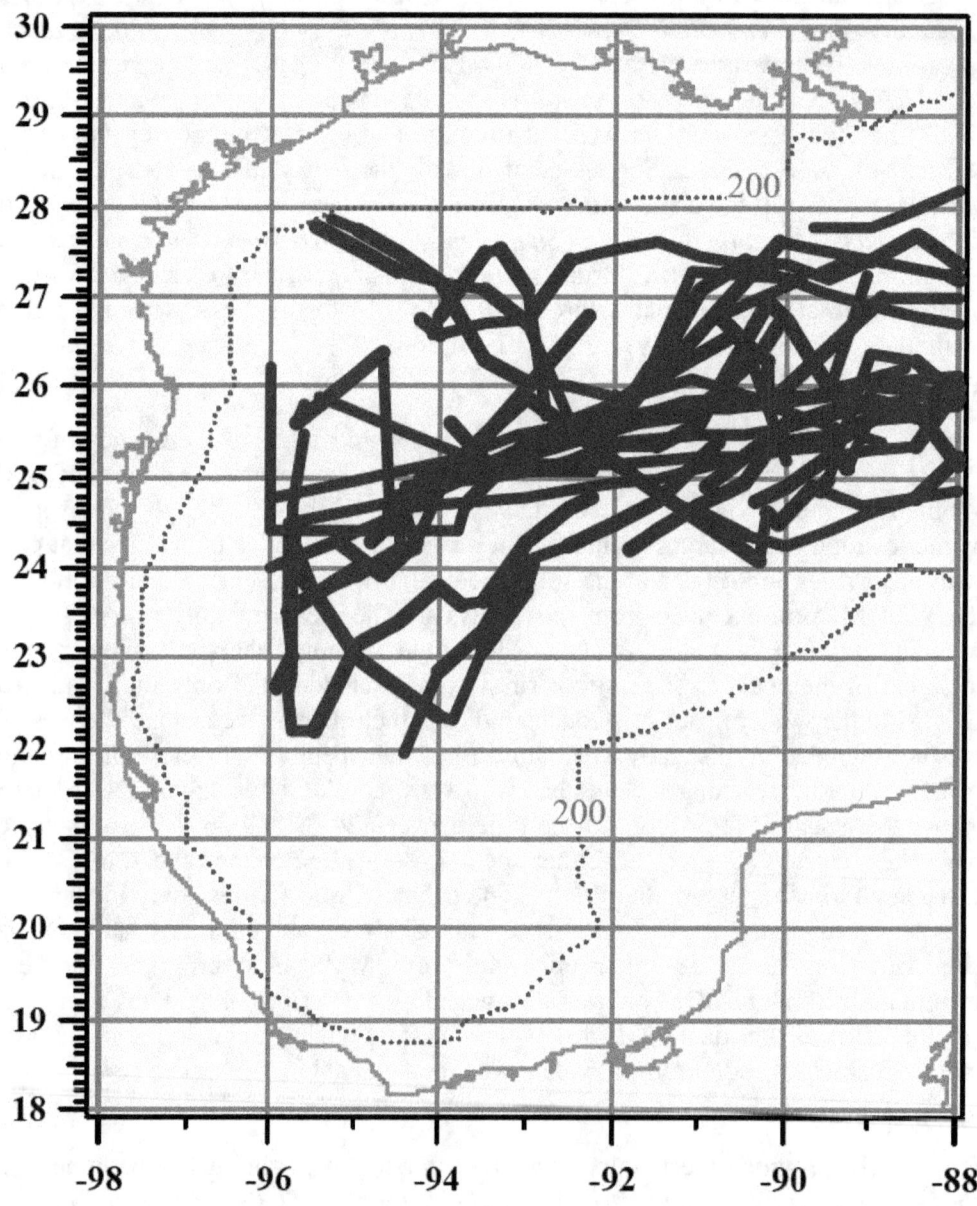

Figure 5.9. Paths of WCRs for the period 1976-2003.

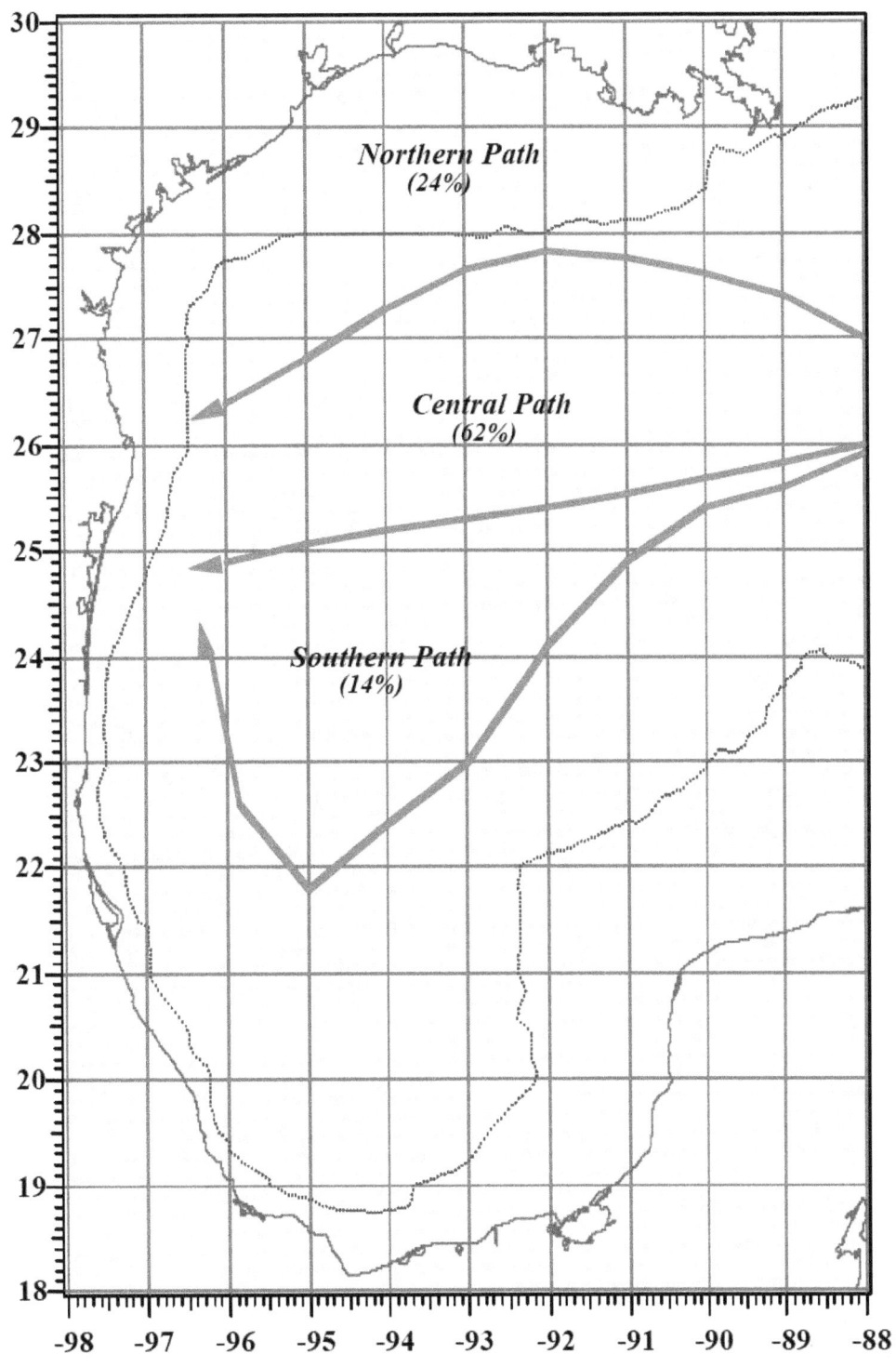

Figure 5.10. Frequency at which WCRs follow each of the three prescribed ring paths (i.e., the Northern Path, the Central Path, and the Southern Path) based data for the period 1976-2003

35

5.3 WCR Speed in the WGOM

5.3.1 Introduction.

Previous studies have indicated that WCRs move through the WGOM at speeds on the order of 5 km/day (Cochrane, 1972; Elliott, 1982; Vukovich and Crissman, 1986). This statistic has been based on studies that examined small number of rings in most cases, but also include a study that examined up to 12 years of data, and involved calculation of the speeds associated with 13 rings. Presently, there is 32 years (i.e., 1972-2003) with which to calculate the speed of WCRs in the WGOM. The ring speed was calculated for 37 major WCRS that existed in the 32-year period. This database should provide better statistic for the ring speed than previously acquire.

5.3.2 Procedure

The speed of the rings was estimated using the available 32-year/37-ring database. It was calculated using successive locations of the center of the ring. As previously indicated, the center of the ring was determined in most cases as the geometric center. When altimetry data were available, the center of the ring was defined as the location of the largest value for the sea-surface height. The west-to-east and south-to-north components of the ring speed were calculated using the longitudes and latitudes, respectively of successive positions of a ring's center, and the ring speed was estimated using the values of the components of the ring speed.

5.3.3 Analysis

The average ring speed over the 32-year period was 4.4 km/day with a standard deviation of ±2.9 km/day. The median ring speed was 4.1 km/day. The average ring speed is slightly smaller than that previously found (i.e., 5 km/day---Cochrane, 1972; Elliott, 1982; Vukovich and Crissman, 1986). *The frequency distribution (Figure 5.11) has a bi-model distribution. The primary mode is found in the interval 4.0-4.9 km/day and the mode for the data is 4.1 km/day. A secondary mode occurred at speeds on the order of 1 km/day.* Ring motion is characterized with periods of "stalls and sprints" (Vukovich and Crissman, 1986; Hamilton et al., 1999). Vukovich and Crissman noted that the stalls are often associated with periods when the rings make major changes in their direction or when their motions is characterized by a tight loop (Figure 5.12). The relatively high-speed motion of the rings, the sprints, occurred when the path of the ring is characterized by quasi-linear motion. The secondary mode in the frequency distribution may be associated with those periods when the path of the rings is characterized by major directional changes or the tight loops.

5.4 Decay of Ring Size

5.4.1 Introduction

As major WCRs move through the WGOM, they have been observed to dissipate (Vukovich and Waddell, 1991; Elliott, 1982; Cochrane 1972). *The size of the rings, which had diameters the order of 300-400 km when they separated from the LC, decrease; have diameters the order of 100-200 km when they reach the western wall; and*

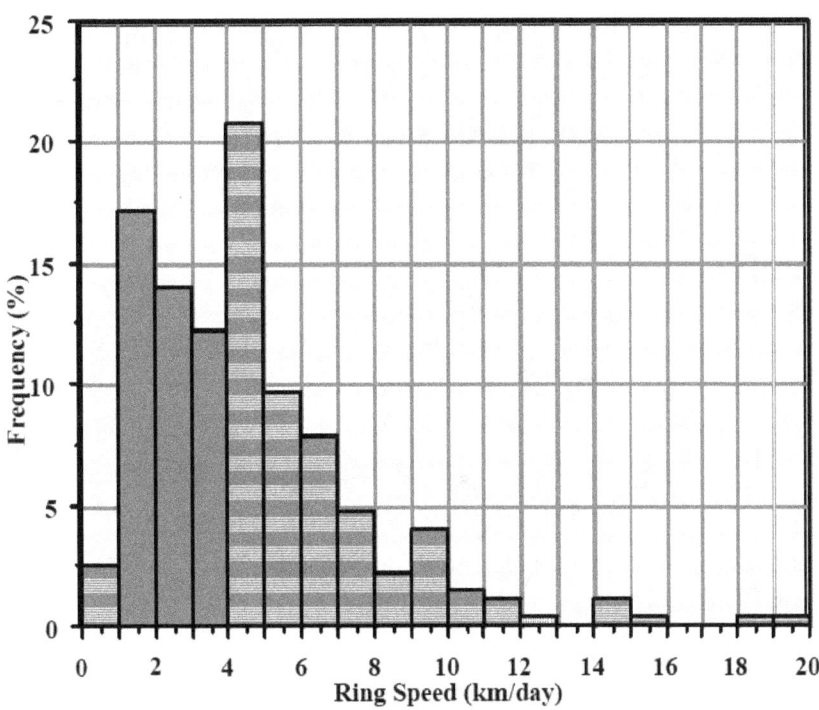

Figure 5.11. Frequency distribution for the speed of WCRs based on data for the period 1972-2003.

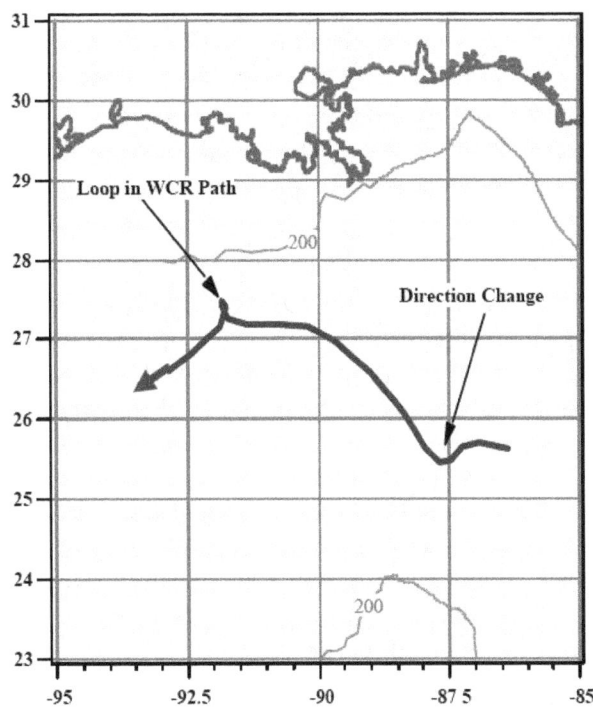

Figure 5.12. Path of a warm ring in the summer of 1983.

an energy transfer often to takes place between the WCRs and CCRs that were found in close proximity to the WCR (Elliott, 1979; Merrill and Morrison, 1981; Merrill and Vazquez, 1983; Brooks, 1984; Hurlburt and Thompson, 1982; Wallcraft, 1986; Smith and O'Brien, 1983; Smith, 1986). Previous studies of the decay of the ring size have used databases as small as 12 years (Vukovich and Crissman, 1986) and as large as 22 years (Herring et al., 1997). For this study, a 28-year (i.e., 1976-2003) database was used to determine the mean rate of decay of the WCRS as they travel through the WGOM.

5.4.2 Procedure

The average decay of the size of WCRs was determined using data for a 28-year period 1976-2003. The ring dissipation was estimated in terms of the month-to-month change of the diameter of a circle whose area was identical to that determined for a major ring that separated from the LC. The area of the ring was calculated for each month using the portrayal of the ring in the monthly frontal analysis. That area was, in many cases, determined as the area of the ellipse that best fit the ring in the analysis, which was then used to estimate the diameter of a circle whose area was identical to that of the ring.

The diameters of the rings were determined for each month during the period when the ring traveled from the EGOM to the western wall in the WGOM. This was done primarily because for certain portions of the period 1976-2003, only satellite SST data were available to track the ring. When the ring became small (i.e., diameters of about 100-200 km), the ring very often could not be detected using the SST. When ocean color and/or altimetry data were available, the rings could be tracked for considerably longer periods. However, for consistency in the period over which the ring diameter was determined for each ring, only data in the period when the ring traveled from the EGOM to the western wall was considered in these calculations. In the 28-year period, 32 rings separated from the LC. However, complete data sets on the evolution of the diameter of the rings could only be obtained for 24 rings. The 8 rings for which complete data sets could not be obtained, were rings that separated from the LC in periods when only satellite SST data were available and detection of the ring size was not possible even with best efforts to enhance the satellite data during image processing.

The time registration in this case was as follows. For the month when the ring separated from the LC, the month was set to zero. For the following months, month = 1, 2, 3, ...etc. By normalizing time relative to the separation month, the average decay of the size of WCRs could be calculated with ease. The average decay of the diameter of WCRs was also normalized relative to the average diameter at the time of separation (i.e., at month = 0, the average normalized ring diameter equaled 1.0).

5.4.3 Analysis

Figure 5.13 shows the variation of the average, normalized diameter of WCRs over an 8-month period. The average diameters were normalized by the average diameter of the ring at the time of separation (i.e., at month = 0, and in this case, the average diameter was 330 km). Data for an eight-month period is only provided in the average because, though data were available for longer periods in some cases, the 8-month period provided a near-uniform number of data points to calculate the average for each month. After the 8th month, the number of data points available to calculate an average decreased markedably. Also shown in the figure is a best-fit Gaussian curve for the data: that is,

$$y = a_o - a_1 \exp[-(a_2 x - a_3)^2];$$

where a_o, a_1, a_2, and a_3 are model coefficients determined by least squares, x is months (i.e., x = 0, 1, 2,....12), and y is the normalized ring diameter. The best-fit curve had an r = 0.97 and average error of about 9 km relative to the observations.

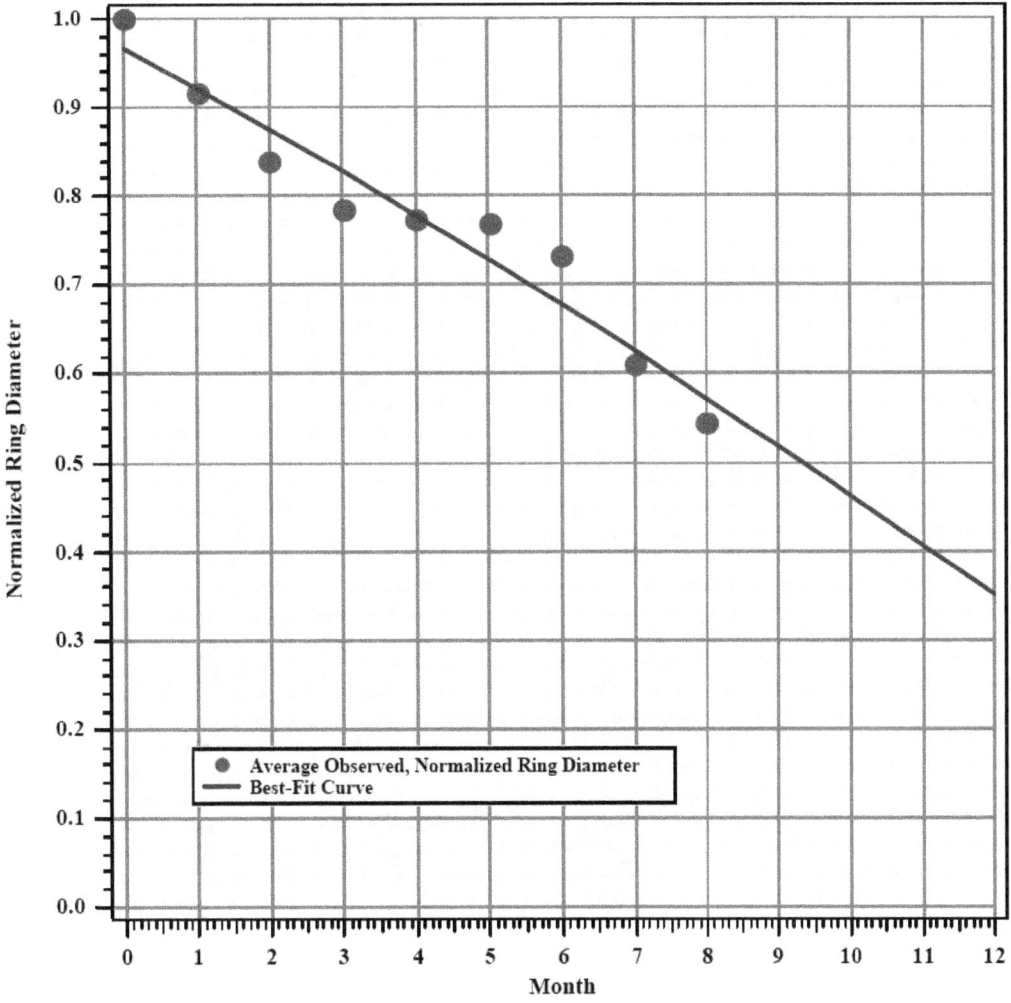

Figure 5.13. Decay of the diameter of WCRs at the surface over time based on data for the period 1976-2003.

According to the observations, the average ring diameter decayed to approximately 55% of it initial size at separation in about 8 months or about 240 days. At that time, the rings that were used in the calculations were located near or at the western wall in the WGOM. There is a 2-month period starting at month = 3 and ending at month = 5 when the ring decay was very weak. After that period, the ring decay was about equivalent or greater than that found in the first three months. It is not clear why the ring decay became weaker in the period month = 3 to month = 5, but this feature, which was associated with momentary ring intensification, appeared to take place for many of the rings used to create this statistic.

According to the best-fit curve, the ring diameter decayed at a rate of about 17 km/month, on average. The actual decay rate was larger than the average indicated by the best-fit curve in the first few months (i.e., the average decay rate in the first 4 months of about 18 km/month) and the last few months (i.e., the average decay rate in the last three month was about 30 km/month). The maximum decay rate in the data was found between month 6 and 7 and was 40 km/day. The best-fit curve did not capture the period of weak decay of the ring noted in the observations in the period month = 3 to month = 5, and indicated that the e-folding took place in approximately 12 months.

5.5 Frequency of WCR Water in the WGOM

5.5.1 Introduction

When WCRs move through the WGOM, the warm water that defined the rings affected a large surface area in the WGOM. The area affected by a single ring is generally largest when the ring enters the WGOM immediately after it has separated from the LC (Figure 5.14), and it is smallest when the ring reaches the western wall of the WGOM, because the size of the ring has decayed to about 55%, on average, of its initial size by the time it has reached that wall (See Section 5.4.3). Some rings expand in the north-south direction when they encounter the western wall (Vukovich and Waddell, 1991). However, the net effect of many rings moving through the WGOM is to have the ring water affect almost the entire northern half of the WGOM (Vukovich and Hamilton, 1990). Some parts of the WGOM will be considerably more affected by ring water than other parts because there are paths that the WCRs will follow when they move through the WGOM more often than others (See Section 5.2). These rings play an important role in the heat and salt budget in the WGOM (Elliott, 1982). Therefore, *an analysis of the frequency of ring water in the WGOM will define areas in the WGOM most affected by ring water and, therefore, where the rings most often directly affect the heat and salt budget in the WGOM.*

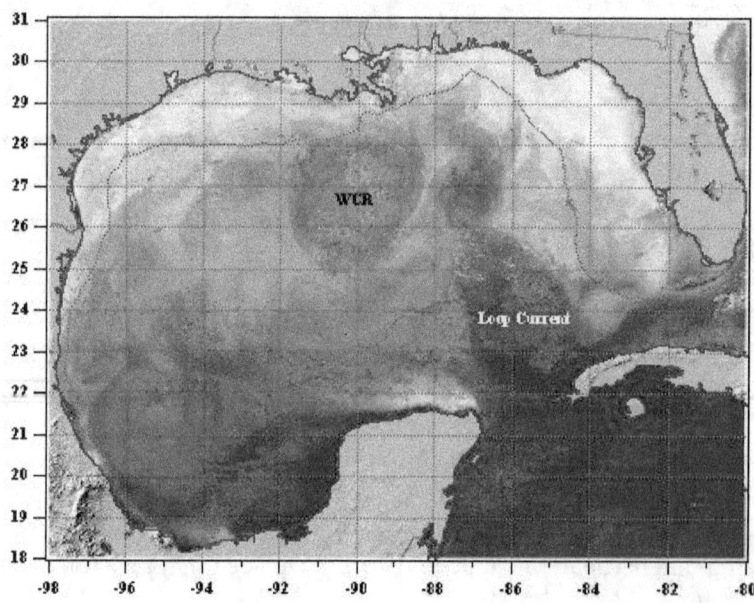

Figure 5.14. NOAA/AVHRR SST image for 23 April 2001 showing a WCR that just separated from the LC.

In this section, a new analysis of the frequency of surface ring water in the WGOM is presented using a 28-year (i.e., 1976-2003) database. Previous studies of the frequency of ring water in the WGOM used a 9-year (1976-1984) database (Vukovich and Hamilton, 1990). Changes in the spatial analysis of the frequency of ring water in the WGOM are expected because the new database covers a period more than 3 times larger.

5.5.2 Procedure

The frequency of surface ring water in the WGOM was created using a 28-year (i.e., 1976-2003) database. As in other cases of this kind, a 0.5° latitude by 0.5° longitude grid was constructed and overlaid onto the frontal analyses. If the water mass associated with a WCR occupied more than 50% of any 0.5° latitude by 0.5° longitude grid square in any given month, then it was assumed that the WCR water mass was present in that grid square at that time. This statistic was derived using monthly frontal analyses that depended primarily on satellite remote sensing data. In the mid 1970s and the late 1980s, only IR SST data were available to create the frontal boundary analyses, and as a result, the WCR fronts could only be determined for about 5 to 8 months in particular years, depending on when the mixed layer developed and was removed. When ocean color and altimetry data were available, WCR fronts could be determined for each month in the year.

5.5.3 Analysis

Figure 5.15 provides the analysis of the spatial frequency of surface water in the WGOM associated with major WCRs that separate from the LC. The magnitude of the frequencies is lower than that for LC water (Figure 4.1) because of the intermittent and non-stationary nature of warm rings. *The maximum frequency (i.e., ~24%) is found near 26° N and 90° W in the eastern portion of the WGOM where the WCRs first enter into the WGOM. There is a zone of high frequency of ring water that stretches along a line oriented west-southwest–east-northeast from about 26° N and 90° W to about 24.75° N and 95° W. The spatial frequency varied along that line from 24% to 16%. This line appears to be parallel to the Central Path of the major WCRs (See Section 5.2), the path that the major rings most often take when they travel through the WGOM. The data indicate that there is a low probability of finding water associated with major rings in the southern portions of the WGOM (i.e., the Bay of Campeche).* This effect is due in part because rings are no longer included in the frontal analysis when the diameter of the rings become on the order of 150 km. The diameter of major rings normally decays to sizes ≤ 150 km soon after the ring reaches the western wall in the WGOM. Rings whose diameters are usually about 150 km or smaller, are the kinds of rings normally found in the Bay of Campeche.

The frequency contours ridge into the northwestern corner of the WGOM. This is because major WCRs are often observed in this region. The region has been called the "graveyard for rings." Rings have been observed to reside in this area for long periods of time, and, at times, become revitalized for short periods of time. It is also possible that an anticyclonic circulation may be generated in that region when the warm water is transported into the northwestern corner of the WGOM by the effect of a ring colliding with the western wall south of the northwest corner. As a result of a ring colliding with the wall south of the northwestern corner, they expand to the north and south, sending ring water into the northwestern corner of the WGOM and producing a weak anticyclonic

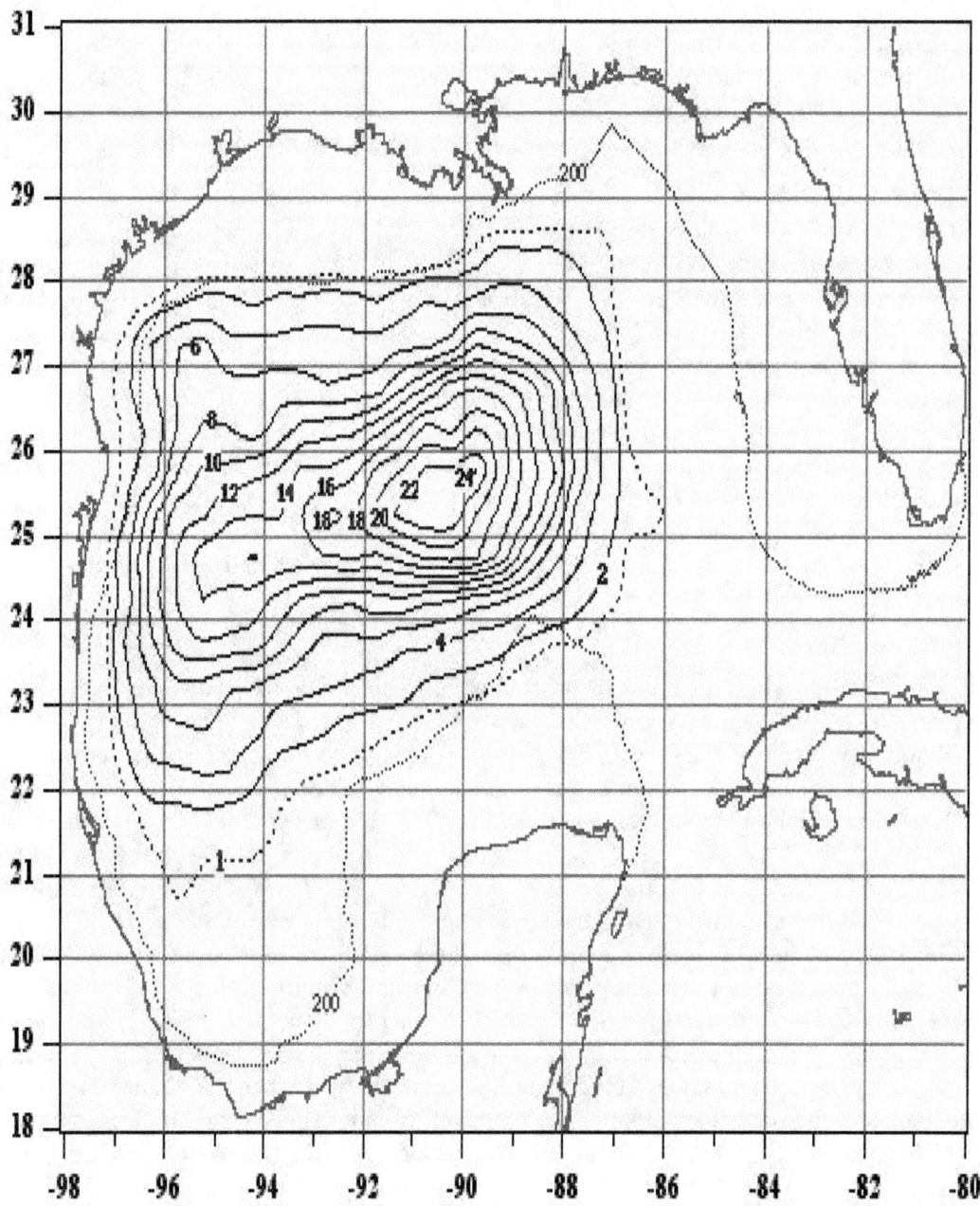

Figure 5.15. The spatial frequency (%) of surface warm water associated with major WCRs that separate from the Loop Current in the WGOM. This analysis is based on a 28-year (1976-2003) database.

circulation in that region (Figure 5.16). Drifter data have clearly shown that in a January 1986 case that the circulation in the northwestern corner was anticyclonic (Vukovich and Waddell, 1991). Sometimes warm water is also transported into the northwestern corner by circulation of a CCR that was located along the western wall just south of the northwestern corner.

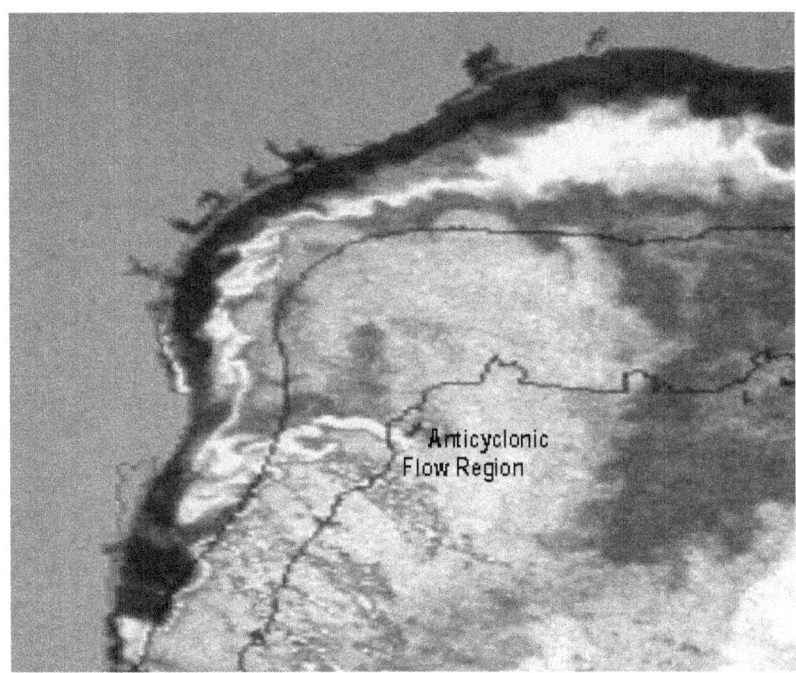

Figure 5.16 NOAA/AVHRR SST image in the northwestern corner of the WGOM for 28 January 1986. Anticyclonic flow was detected in the northwest corner of the GOM (See Vukovich and Waddell, 1991).

5.6 Frequency of the Position of WCR Centers in the GOM

5.6.1 Introduction

Major WCRs separate from the LC about once every 11 months, on average, though the actual frequency is highly variable. These rings move into the WGOM where they dissipate. However, minor WCRs (i.e., WCRs that are smaller and/or that do not have deep vertical structure) also separate from the LC. Some of these rings move into the WGOM, while others stay in the NEGOM. The minor rings dissipate quickly (i.e., in about 2 to 5 months), but play a role in the heat and salt balance and on the circulation in the GOM. Warm rings are believed to be a major contributor to the transport in the WGOM and the maintenance of an anticyclonic cell along the western boundary of the GOM (Brooks, 1984; Nowlin and McLellan, 1967; Elliott 1982). The anticyclonic circulation associated with WCRs has a profound effect on the surface trajectories in the WGOM (Hamilton et al., 1999; Lewis and Kirwan, 1985). Obviously, information on the persistence of WCRs in the GOM is vital to our understanding of the circulation in the GOM. In this section, an analysis of the spatial frequency of the location of the centers of WCRs is presented. This analysis was created using a 27-year (i.e., 1977-2003) database.

5.6.2 Procedure

The analysis of the spatial frequency of the location of the centers of WCRs was created using a 27-year (i.e., 1977-2003) database. For the period 1977-1991, the location of the centers of WCRs was derived from the frontal analyses discussed in Section 3.0. The frontal analyses for that period were based, for the most part, on satellite SST data and CZCS ocean color data when they were available. Minor rings were included in the

43

frontal analyses for this period when they could be detected and for as long as they were detectable. In the mid 1970s and the late 1980s, only SST data were available to create the frontal boundary analyses, and as a result, the WCRs could only be determined for about 5 to 8 months in particular years, depending on when the mixed layer developed and was removed. Furthermore, minor rings could only be detected during this period in the first month or two after separation from the LC. For the period 1992-2003, the database used for this analysis also included of satellite altimetry data. When satellite altimetry data was included in this analysis, data were available for this analysis each month in the year. The altimetry data provided daily analyses of all rings (i.e., either WCRs or CCRs) in the GOM (Figure 5.17).

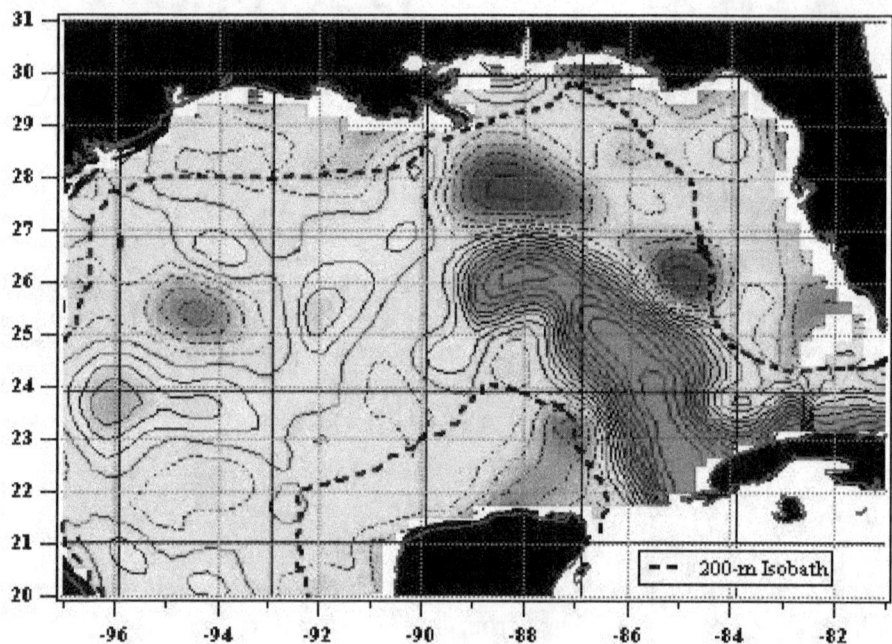

Figure 5.17. Analysis of the sea-surface height in the GOM from satellite altimetry data for 15 April 2003. The red/yellow areas with solid lines define areas with large values of sea-surface height and the blue areas with dashed lines are areas with low values of sea-surface height.

A 1° latitude by 1° longitude grid was constructed and overlaid onto the frontal analyses or the satellite altimetry analyses. If a WCR center occupied a 1° latitude by 1° longitude grid square, then it was assumed that the ring center was present in that grid square for that month. The center of the ring was defined as the location of the largest value for the sea-surface height in the altimetry data or the geometric center in the frontal analysis created using SST and/or ocean color data. When the largest-valued closed contour that defined the center of the ring in the analysis of the altimetry data encompassed a broad area, the geometric center of the closed contour was used as the center of the ring. *NOTA BENE*: this analysis took into account major and minor rings, including major rings for periods after they reached the western wall. Minor rings were detected at most three (3) months after they separated from the LC using SST and/or ocean color data. Major rings could be detected at most four months after they reached the western wall using those data. Major and Minor rings could be detected until they dissipated using altimeter data.

5.6.3 Analysis

The magnitude of the spatial frequencies of the location of the centers of WCRs (Figure 5.18) is smaller than that for ring water (Figure 5.15). The surface water associated with a single ring sweeps out an area as the ring moves through the WGOM, which will affect many grid squares; whereas the center of a WCR is a single point in space that will affect a single grid square at any point in time and only a small number of grid squares as the ring moves westward.

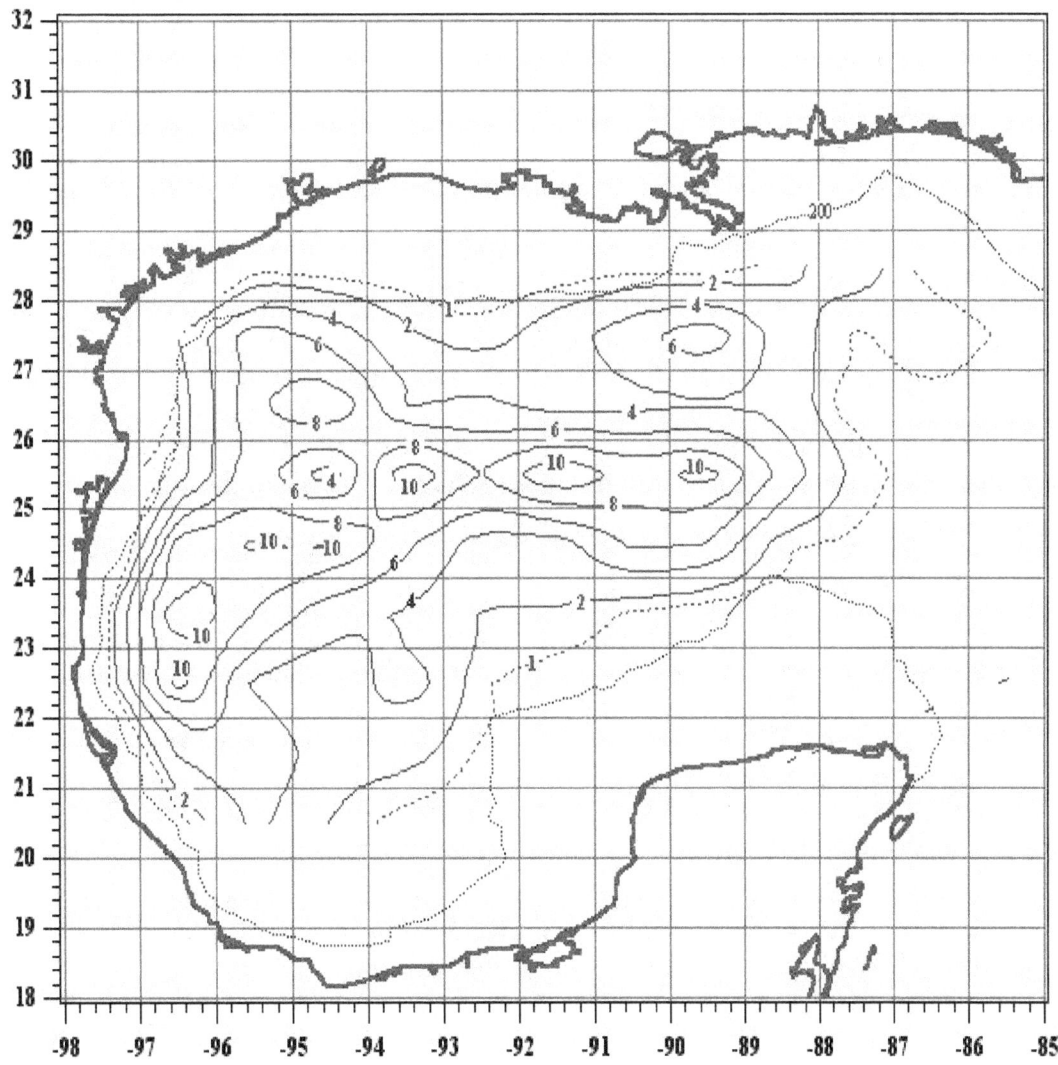

Figure 5.18. Spatial frequency (%) for the location of WCR centers using a 27-year (1977-2003) database.

The analysis shows an east-west zone of high spatial frequency for the ring centers located in the 25° N-26° N latitude belt from 88° W to 94° W. Multiple centers are found in that zone, and the maximum frequency in that zone is about 12%, which is a little more than one event every year, on average. One event every year might be considered rather high considering that major rings do not necessarily separate from the LC that often (See Section 5.1) nor is the path of the rings always in this area (See Section 5.2). There are a couple of reasons for this frequency. In periods when the movement of major rings slowed because they were either changing direction or their motion formed a loop (See Section 5.3), the ring, in some case, did not move over a great distance and occupied the same grid square for more than a one-month period. Another reason for the one event every year is the fact that minor rings were included in the analysis. Minor rings move slowly, are often quasi-stationary, and dissipate quickly. Under these conditions, minor rings can make a serious contribution in the eastern part of the analysis.

North of the eastern part of the east-west zone of high frequency is a secondary center of relatively high spatial frequency for the ring centers (i.e., located at around 27.5° N and 89.5° W). The maximum frequency in this center is about 7%, which is about one event every 17 months. In this region, both major and minor rings made serious contributions to the spatial frequency. *This center is important because rings located in this region can make a marked impact on the circulation on the Louisiana shelf and the slope in that region.*

Immediately west of the east-west zone of high frequency is a center of low spatial frequency (i.e., located at around 25.5° N and 94.5° W). The minimum frequency in that center is about 3%, which is about one event every 4 years. The reason for the minimum in this region is not completely clear. In the next section (Section 6.1), it will be shown that this area is an area where CCRs are often found. The dominance of CCRs in this region may inhibit WCRs from invading the region. WCRs are normally much smaller when they reach the western wall of the WGOM and have about the same dimensions as CCRs in this area, so that a CCR is just as likely to occupy a position near the western wall as a WCR. The data on ring paths in Section 5.2 would suggests that very few major rings move into this region when they move across the WGOM to the western wall.

North and south of the low frequency area discussed in the last paragraph are areas of relatively high frequency for ring centers. The area to the north is in the northwestern corner of the GOM, which region, as previously discussed, has been called the graveyard for rings. Rings have been observed to reside in this area for long periods of time; and at times, those rings have become revitalized for a period of time due to interactions with other WCRs (Vukovich and Waddell, 1991) and/or CCRs. The maximum frequency in that area is about 10%, which is about one event every year.

The zone of relatively high frequency in the area to the south of the low frequency area is located near the western boundary of the GOM and the maximum frequency in that area is about 12%, which is a little greater than one event every 12 months. This feature was created by a large number of major rings that reached the western wall, that were reduced considerably in size at that time, and that moved southward after reaching the western wall. Considerably more rings moved southward than northward after they reached the western wall. The fact that there is a persistence of WCR centers in this area supports the notion that these rings may be major contributors to the transport in the WGOM and the maintenance of an anticyclonic cell along the western boundary of the GOM (Brooks, 1984; Nowlin and McLellan, 1967; Elliott 1982).

6. COLD CORE RINGS

6.1 Frequency of the Position of CCR Centers in the GOM

6.1.1 Introduction

CCRs are an integral part of the dynamics in the GOM. They are generally small in size (i.e., diameters on the order of 100 km). They have been observed in the GOM along the boundary of the LC (Vukovich et al., 1979a and b; O'Connor, 1981; Vukovich and Maul, 1985; Vukovich, 1986, Vukovich, 1988a), off the Dry Tortugas (Maul and Herman, 1985, Vukovich, 1988b), and on the boundary of WCRs (Elliott, 1979; Merrill and Morrison, 1981, Merrill and Vazquez, 1983, Brooks, 1984; Kelley and Brooks, 1986; Kelley et al., 1986; Kelley et al., 1987; Vukovich and Waddell, 1991). Their circulation can influence the water mass characteristics on the West Florida Shelf (See Figure 4.8 in Section 4) and in the northeastern GOM (See Figures 4.5 and 4.7 in Section 4). CCRs have been observed to develop or intensify along the northwestern portions of the LC boundary when the LC penetrates deep into the EGOM (i.e., when the northern boundary of the LC is found as far north as 27° N) [Vukovich, 1988a]. They move along the LC boundary in the direction of the flow from the Yucatan Strait to the Straits of Florida. They have been observed to be associated with the separation of a WCR from the LC (Figure 6.1) [Vukovich et al., 1979a; Vukovich, 1988a]. The production of CCRs on the boundary of WCRs is considered part of the dissipation process associated with WCRs (Cushman-Roisin, 1987; Smith 1986). They move along the boundary of the WCRs in a clockwise manner associated with the anticyclonic flow in the WCRs. CCRs are highly mobile. However, if these rings were persistent in regions of the GOM, the circulation associated with these rings can potentially influence local water characteristics and local surface trajectories. In this section, an analysis of the spatial frequency of the location of the centers of CCRs is presented, which will provide information on the persistence of these rings in certain areas in the GOM. This analysis was created using a 12-year (i.e., 1992-2003) database.

6.1.2 Procedure

The procedure for creating the analysis of the spatial frequency of the location of the centers of CCRs was identical to that used to create the analysis of the spatial frequency of the location of the centers of WCRs. The analysis was created using a 12-year (i.e., 1992-2003) database. The database used for this analysis was entirely made up of satellite altimetry data. The altimetry data provided daily analyses of all rings (i.e., either WCRs or CCRs) in the GOM (See Figure 5.17 in Section 5). A 1° latitude by 1° longitude grid was constructed and overlaid satellite altimetry analyses. If the center of a CCR occupied a 1° latitude by 1° longitude grid square in a given month, then it was assumed that the ring center was present in that grid square for that month. The center of the ring was defined as the location of the smallest value for the sea-surface height. When the smallest-valued closed contour that defined the center of the ring in the altimetry analysis encompassed a broad area, the geometric center of the closed contour was used as the center of the ring. Since this analysis was dependent on only satellite altimetry data, data were available for this analysis each month in the year.

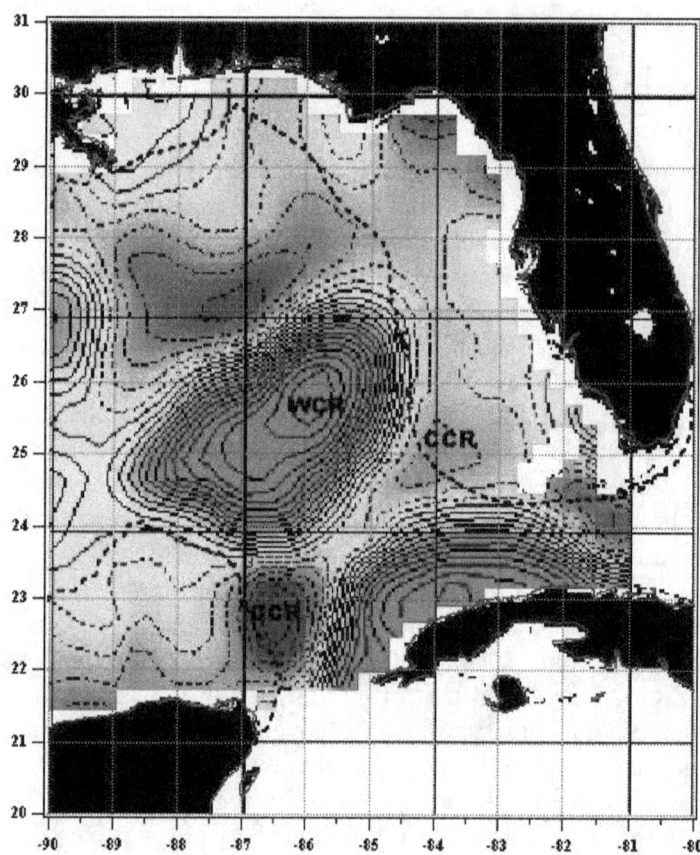

Figure 6.1. TOPEX/ERS sea-surface height image for 1 October 2003.
CCRs are found off the Campeche Bank to the southwest of
the WCR and off the West Florida Shelf to the southeast of the
WCR. This configuration of rings is a common occurrence
with WCR separation.

6.1.3 Analysis

Figure 6.2 provides the analysis of the spatial frequency of the location of the centers of CCRs using the 12-year (i.e., 1992-2003) satellite altimetry database. *In the EGOM (i.e., the region east of 90° W in the GOM), the analysis shows a northwest-southeast oriented zone of relatively high frequency of CCR centers, having two centers of high frequency. The center in the northwestern part of that zone (i.e., the center located at about 27.5° N and 88.5° W) has a maximum frequency of about 30%, which corresponds to about 3-4 events per year.* This center of maximum frequency is found in an area of the EGOM where CCRs have been noted to either develop or intensify on the boundary of the LC (Vukovich,1988a). When CCRs develop or intensify on the boundary of the LC, they have been observed to become quasi-stationary for a period of time (e.g., one-four months), before the move downstream, so that a frequency of 3-4 events per year does not necessarily mean 3-4 individual CCRs, but that a CCR may have persisted for 3-4 months in a year. If a WCR separates after the CCR develops or intensifies on the boundary of the LC in this area, then the CCR may also contribute to this center of maximum frequency a number of times also as it moves along the boundary of the WCR while the WCR moves westward into the WGOM. *It should also be noted that because of the high frequency with which these CCRs are found in this region, they often interact with the shelf off the Louisiana and Alabama coast, transporting shelf water into the deep Gulf* (Figure 6.3).

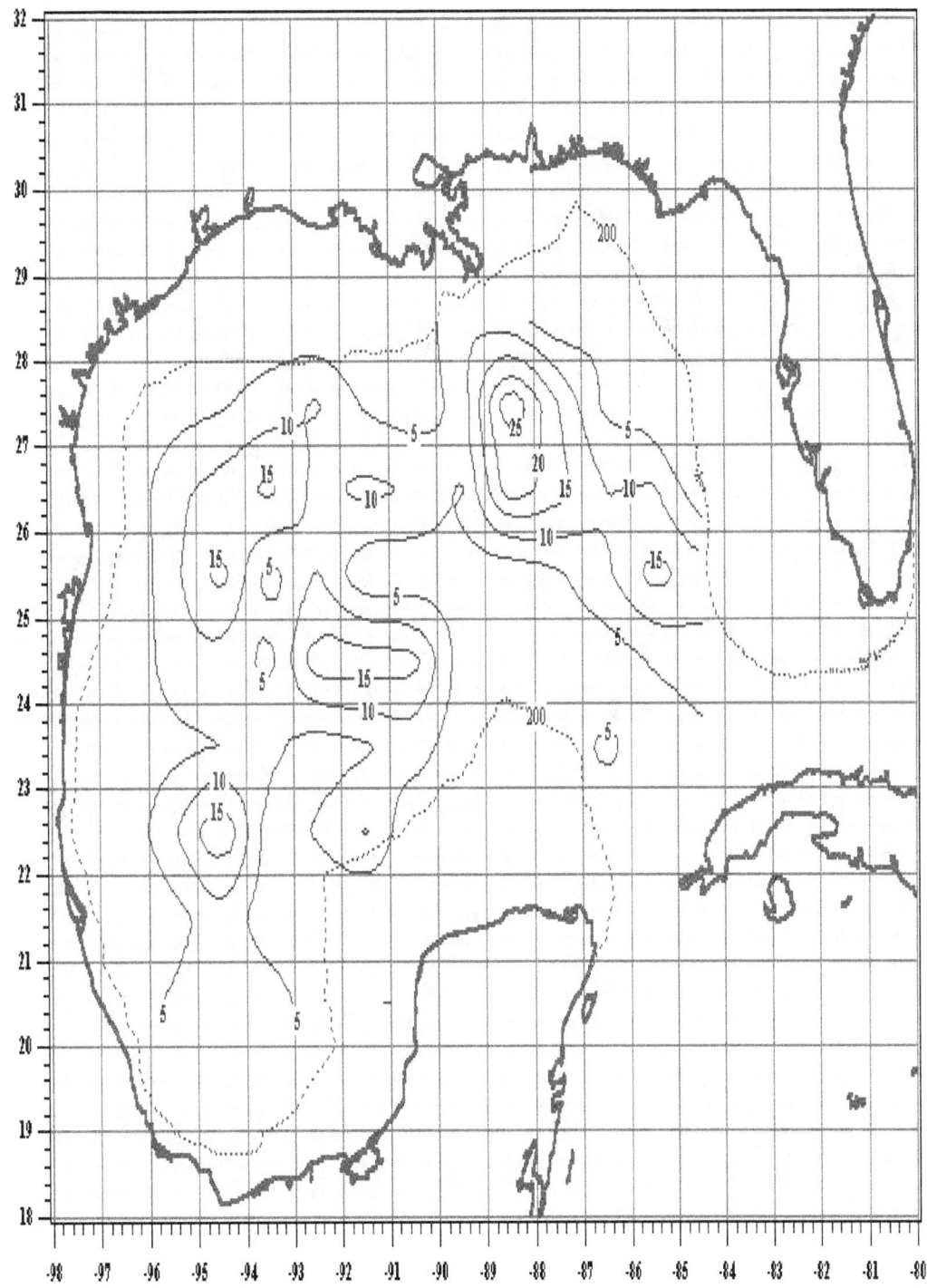

Figure 6.2. Analysis of the spatial frequency (%) for the location of CCR centers using a 12-year (1992-2003) database.

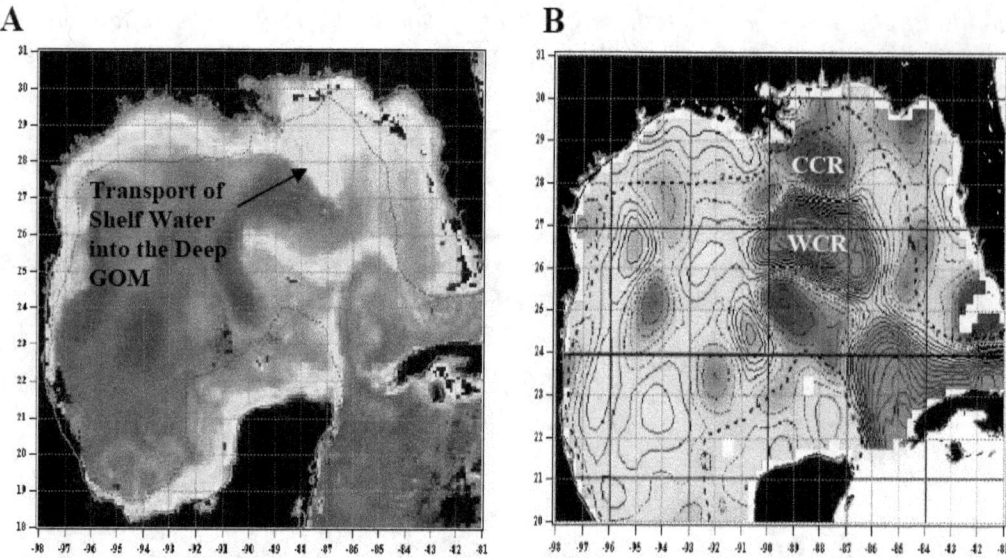

Figure 6.3. Interaction of a CCR on the northwestern boundary of a WCR/LC in mid-September 2004. (A) MODIS ocean color image and (B) SSH from the JASON Altimeter.

The center in the southeastern portion of that zone (i.e., the center located at about 25.5˚ N and 85.5˚ W) has a maximum frequency of about 17%, which corresponds to about 2 events per year. This center is found in an area where CCRs have been observed off the Dry Tortugas (Maul and Herman, 1985, Vukovich, 1988b) and where they have been observed to be associated with the separation of a WCR from the LC (Vukovich et al., 1979a; Vukovich, 1988a). These CCR have been known to persist in that location for 1-2 months at a time, so that, as in the previous case, a frequency of about 2 events per year does not necessarily mean 2 separate CCRs, but that a single CCR may have persisted in that area for 2 months in a year.

In the WGOM, the analysis shows four major centers of relatively high frequency of CCR centers: one at 24.5K N and 91.5˚ W; one at 26.5˚ N and 93.5˚ W; one at 25.5˚ N, 94.5˚ N; and one at 22.5˚ N and 94.5˚ W. The center located at 24.5K N and 91.5˚ W has a maximum frequency of about 18.4 %, that at 26.5˚ N and 93.5˚ W has a maximum frequency of about 16.3%, that at 25.5˚ N and 94.5˚ W has a maximum frequency of about 17%, and that at 22.5˚ N and 94.5˚ W has a maximum frequency of about 20.6%. In each case, the maximum frequency corresponds to about 1-2 events per year. These centers are produced by CCRs associated with a number of process events that take place in the WGOM. *These CCRs are most often associated with major WCRs that separate from the LC, and they are found on the boundary of the WCRs* (Elliott, 1979; Merrill and Morrison, 1981; Merrill and Vazquez, 1983; Brooks, 1984; Kelley and Brooks, 1986; Kelley et al., 1986; Kelley et al., 1987; and Vukovich and Waddell, 1991). The major WCRs that move through the WGOM, generally enter the WGOM north of the center of maximum frequency for the CCRs located at 24.5K N and 91.5˚ W in about 80% of the cases, which suggests that the CCRs that contribute to that center are most probably found on the southern boundary of those WCRs. The CCRs that contribute to the centers of maximum frequency that are located near the western wall of the WGOM (i.e., those located at 26.5˚ N, 93.5˚ W; 25.5˚ N, 94.5˚ N; and 22.5˚ N, 94.5˚ W) are associated with the CCRS that are observed with a major WCR when it reaches the western wall. A ring pair (i.e., a WCR and a CCR, which are about the same size) is often observed together at the western wall and the ring pair has been linked to the dissipation of the WCR (Cushman-Roisin, 1987 and Smith 1986). Sometimes, the CCR in the pair is found to the north of the WCR, and sometimes it is found to the south. It must be made clear, however, that CCRs associated with WCRs are major contributors to the development of these three centers of relatively high frequency of CCR centers, but they are not the only contributors. CCRs that are not directly associated with WCRs have been observed in these regions and have contributed to the development of these centers. In most cases, these CCRs are unique, non-recurring events.

7.0 SUMMARY OF FINDINGS

The following is an outline of the major findings from this study:

Loop Current

The LC front reached 28° N latitude in the EGOM only about 5% of the time and 27° N about 20% of the time. About 80% of the LC's orientation angles are between 0° (a north-south orientation) and 30° (a north-northwest to south-southeast orientation), which represent a stable orientation for the LC; that is, ring separation is not expected anytime soon. Less than 20% of the LC's orientation angles are greater than 30°, which represent an unstable mode for the LC and ring separation is usually expected soon.

Isolated warm pools of LC water were found throughout the region north of 26° N in the EGOM. The highest frequency for the warm pools in the EGOM was about 14% and it was found near 27° N and 85° W, just west of the shelf break for the WFS. This center of high frequency was created, for the most part, as a result of many cases in which there was transport of warm LC water by the circulation associated with CCRs located on the boundary of the LC.

Intrusions of LC water onto the WFS are, for the most part, due to transport associated with a CCR located on the eastern boundary of the LC. Most of these intrusions are found south of 27° N and between the shelf break and 83° W. The maximum frequency is about 12%, which corresponds to about one event per year.

Warm Core Rings

The frequency distribution for the period for separation of major rings from the LC had a bi-model distribution with modes at 6 and 11 months and a range of 5 to 19 months. The average period was 11 months and the standard deviation was ± 4 months. The average period was identical to one of the modes of the frequency distribution, suggesting that 11 months might be the most characteristic period for eddy shedding. The average period did not change substantially over the 10-year period 1994-2003, remaining at about 11 months. A high frequency of ring separation was found in March, and no rings were observed to separate from the LC in December.

The period with the most significant variance in the variance-preserved spectrum of the LC northern boundary variations was 12 months, suggesting that 12 months might be the most characteristic period for eddy shedding based on these data. The most significant variance showed a one-month variation over the last ten years (1994-2003), presumably a result of the year-to-year variability in the eddy-shedding period.

In terms of the path that the WCRs take through the WGOM, the Central Path had the highest frequency (62%). The Northern Path had the next highest frequency (24%), and the least likely trajectory for the WCRs was the Southern Path (18%). The average speed of the WCRs through the WGOM was 4.4 km/day with a standard deviation of ± 2.9 km/day. The frequency distribution of WCR speeds had a bi-model distribution with modes in the increments of 4.0 to 4.9 km/day and 1.0 to 1.9 km/day.

WCRs decayed, on average, to about 55% of their initial size in about 8 months. There was a period of about two months, starting at the fourth month after separation of the ring, when the decay rate decreased significantly.

The maximum frequency of WCR water in the WGOM occurred near 25°N and 90° W and was 24%. There was a zone of relatively high frequency of WCR water in the WGOM that stretched along a west-southwest--east-northeast line from 26° N and 90° W to 24.75° N and 95° W where the frequency varied from 24% to 16%, which appeared to be associated with the Central Path of the major rings through the WGOM. The frequency contours for WCR water ridged into the northwest corner of the WGOM where major WCRs are often observed.

An east-west zone of relatively high frequency of WCRs was found in the WGOM in the 25-26° N latitude belt from 88° W to 94° W in which the maximum frequency was about 12%, corresponding to little more than one event per year. A secondary region of relatively high frequency of WCRs was found at around 27.4° N and 89.6° W for which minor rings played a significant role. Another region of relatively high frequency of WCR was found in the northwest corner of the WGOM, where, as previously indicated, major rings are often observed. Another region of relatively high frequency of WCRs was found near the western wall between 22° N and 25° N, in which the maximum frequency was about 12%, corresponding to little more than one event per year. This region supports the notion that WCRs may be major contributors to transport in the WGOM and the maintenance of an anticyclonic cell along the GOM's western boundary (Brooks, 1984; Nowlin and McLellan, 1967; Elliott 1982). In the WGOM, WCRs play an important role in the heat and salt balance (Elliot, 1982). These data indicate that WCRs have their most significant effect on the heat and salt balance north of 24° N.

Cold Core Rings

In the EGOM, there was a northwest-southeast oriented zone of relatively high frequency for CCRs, having two centers of maximum. The northwestern center was located at around 27.5° N and 88.5° W, which is in an area where CCRs have been previously found to intensify and/or develop (Vukovich, 1988a), and the maximum frequency in this area was about 30% (the highest frequency noted for any kind of ring—warm or cold), which corresponds to about 3-4 events per year. The southeastern center was located at around 25.5° N and 85.5° W, which is in the Dry Tortugas region where CCRs have been previously noted (Maul and Herman, 1985 and Vukovich 1988a and b), and the maximum frequency in this area was about 17%, which corresponds to about 2 events per year. In the WGOM, four region of relatively high frequency for CCRs were found. The maximum frequency in these regions varied from 16-20%, corresponding to about 1-2 events per year.

This study showed that in the EGOM, CCRs, which are very persistent and/or numerous in that area, play an important role in redistributing heat and salt. They accounted for a large portion of the development of isolated pools LC water in the EGOM and for all intrusions of LC water onto the WFS through the transport associated with their circulation.

8. REFERENCES

Brooks, P.A. 1984. Current and hydrographic variability in the northwestern Gulf of Mexico. J. Geophys. Res. 89(C5): 8022-8032.

Cochrane, J.C. 1972. Separation of an anticyclone and subsequent developments of the Loop Current (1969). In: Capurro, L.R.A. and J.L. Reid (editors). Contributions on the physical oceanography of the Gulf of Mexico. Houston, TX: Gulf Publishing. Pp. 91-106.

Cushman-Roisin, B. 1987. Exact analytical solution for an elliptical vortices of the shallow water equations. Tellus 39A: 235-244.

Elliott B. A. 1979. Anticyclonic rings and the energetics of the circulation in the Gulf of Mexico. Ph.D. dissertation, Texas A&M University, College Station, TX. 188 pp.

Elliott B. A. 1982. Anticyclonic rings in the Gulf of Mexico. J. Phys. Oceanogr. 12(11): 1292-1309.

Hamilton, P., G.S. Fargion, and D.C. Biggs. 1999. Loop Current eddy paths in the Western Gulf of Mexico. J. Phys. Oceanogr. 29(6): 1180-1207.

He, R. and R.H. Weisberg. 2003. A Loop Current intrusion case study on the West Florida Shelf. J. Phys. Oceanogr. 33(2): 465-477.

Herring, H.J., M. Inoue, G.L. Mellor, C.N.K.Mooers, P.P. Niiler, R C. Patchen, R.C. Perez, F.M. Vukovich, and W. J. Wiseman. 1997. Coastal ocean modeling in the Gulf of Mexico. U.S. Dept. of the Interior, Minerals Management Service, Herndon, Va. Report 115. 156 pp.

Hurlburt, H.E. and J.D. Thompson. 1982. The dynamics of the Loop Current and shed eddies in a numerical experiment of the Gulf of Mexico. In: Nihoul, J.C.J. (editor). Hydrodynamics of semi-enclosed seas, New York, Elsevier: Pp. 243-298.

Jacobs, G.A. and R. Leben. 1990. Loop Current eddy shedding estimates using Geosat altimeter data. Geophys. Res. Lett. 17: 2385-2388.

Kelley, F.J. and D.A. Brooks. 1986. Observations of eddy interaction with topography in the western Gulf of Mexico. EOS 64(44).

Kelley, F.J., D.A. Brooks, A. Vazquez, and G.S.E. Lagerloeff. 1986. Observations of a warm-core Loop Current eddy in the western Gulf of Mexico. EOS, 67(16).

Kelley, F.J., A.M. Vasquez de la Cerda, and D.A. Brooks. 1987. El origen de los remolinas oceanicas en la frontera entre USA y Mexico. Proceedings of the 2nd

Reunion Indicativade Actividades Regionales Relacionadas con la Oceanografia (Golfo de Mexico y Mar Caribe Mexicanos) Comision Intersecretarial de Investigacion Oceanografia, Veracruz, Mexico.

Lewis, J.K. and A.D. Kirwan Jr. 1985. Some observations of eddy topography and ring-ring interaction in the Gulf of Mexico. J. Geophys. Res. 90(C5): 9089-9096.

Maul, G.A., D.A. Mayer, and A.R. Baig. 1985. Comparisons between a continuous 3-year current-meter observations of the sill of the Yucatan Strait, satellite measurements of the Gulf Loop Current area, and regional sea level. J. Geophys. Res. 90(C5): 9017-9028.

Maul, G.A. and A. Herman. 1985. Mean dynamic topography of the Gulf of Mexico with applications to satellite imagery. Mar. Geodesy 9(1): 27-43.

Maul, G.A. and F.M. Vukovich. 1993. Aspects of the relationship between the sub-seasonal cycle of the Gulf of Mexico Loop Current and the Straits of Florida volume transport. J. Phys. Oceanogr. 23(5): 785-796.

Merrill, W.J. and J.M. Morrison. 1981. On the circulation of the western Gulf of Mexico with observations from April 1978. J. Geophys. Res. 86: 4181-4185.

Merrill, W.J. and A.M. Vazquez. 1983. Observations of the changing mesoscale circulation patterns in the western Gulf of Mexico. J. Geophys. Res. 88: 7721-7723.

Nowlin, W.D., Jr. and H.J. McLellan. 1967. A characterization of Gulf of Mexico waters in winter. J. Mar. Res. 25: 29-59.

O'Connor, D. 1981. The thermal anomaly in the Gulf of Mexico observed during May 1980. Gulf Stream 4: 6-8.

Oey, L., H. Lee, and W.J. Schmitz, Jr. 2003. Effects of winds and Caribbean eddies on the frequency of Loop Current eddy shedding: A numerical study. J. Geophys. Res. 108: 3324-3335.

Smith, D.C. 1986. A numerical study of Loop Current eddy interaction with topography in the western Gulf of Mexico. J. Phys. Oceanogr. 16: 1260-1272.

Smith, D.C. and J.J. O'Brien. 1983. The interaction of a two layer isolated mesoscale eddy with topography. J. Phys. Oceanogr. 13: 1681-1697.

Sturges, W. 1995. The frequency of ring separation from the Loop Current. J. Phys. Oceanogr. 24: 1647-1651.

Sturges, W. 1992. The spectrum of Loop Current variability from gappy data. J. Phys. Oceanogr. 22: 1245-1256.

Sturges, W. and J.C. Evans. 1983. On the variability of the Loop Current in the Gulf of Mexico. J. Mar. Res. 41: 639-653.

Sturges, W. and R. Leben. 2000. Frequency of ring separation from the Loop Current in the Gulf of Mexico. J. Phys. Oceanogr. 30: 1245-1256.

Sutyrin, G.G., G.D. Rowe, L.M. Rothstein, and I. Ginis. 2003. Baroclinic eddy interation with continental slopes and shelves. J. Phys. Oceanogr. 33: 283-291.

Vukovich, F.M. 1995. An updated evaluation of the Loop Currents eddy shedding frequency. J. Geophys. Res. 100(C5): 8655-8659.

Vukovich, F.M. 1988a. Loop Current boundary variations. J. Geophys. Res. 93(C12): 15,585-15,591.

Vukovich, F.M. 1988b. On the formation of elongated cold perturbations off the Dry Tortugas. J. Phys. Oceanogr. 18(7): 1051-1059.

Vukovich, F.M. 1986. Aspects of the behavior of cold perturbations in the Eastern Gulf of Mexico: A case study. J. Phys. Oceanogr. 16(1): 175-188.

Vukovich, F.M. and P. Hamilton. 1990. New atlas of front locations in the Gulf of Mexico. In: Geo-Marine, Inc., comp. Proceedings: Tenth annual Gulf of Mexico information transfer meeting, December 1989. U.S. Dept. of the Interior, Minerals Management Service, Gulf of Mexico OCS Region, New Orleans, La. OCS Study MMS 90-0027. pp. 163-168.

Vukovich, F.M. and E. Waddell. 1991. Interaction of a warm ring with the western slope in the Gulf of Mexico. J. Phys. Oceanogr. 22(7): 1062-1074.

Vukovich, F.M. and B.W. Crissman. 1986. Aspects of warm rings in the Gulf of Mexico. J. Geophys. Res. 91(C2): 2645-2660.

Vukovich, F.M. and G.A. Maul. 1985. Cyclonic eddies in the eastern Gulf of Mexico. J. Phys. Oceanogr. 15(1): 105-117.

Vukovich, F.M., B.W. Crissman, M. Bushnell, and W.J. King. 1979a. Some aspects of the oceanography of the Gulf of Mexico using satellite and in-situ data. J. Geophys. Res. 84(C12): 7749-7768.

Vukovich, F.M., B.W. Crissman, and D. Erlich. 1979b. Sea-surface temperature variability analysis of potential OTEC sites in the eastern Gulf of Mexico utilizing satellite data. NOAA Contract No. 03-78 B01-72. 37 pp.

Vukovich, F.M., B.W. Crissman, M. Bushnell, and W.J. King. 1978. Sea-surface temperature variability analysis of potential OTEC sites utilizing satellite data. DOE Contract No. EG-77-C-05-5444, NTIS No ORO54441. 46 pp.

Wallcraft, A.J. 1986. Gulf of Mexico circulation modeling study, annual progress report: year 2. Progress Report by JAYCOR to the U.S. Department of the Interior, Minerals Management Service, Metairie, LA, MMS Contract 14-12-0001-30073. 94 pp.

Wang, D., L. Oey, T. Ezer, and P. Hamilton. 2003. Near-surface currents in DeSoto Canyon (1997-1999): Comparison of current meters, satellite observations, and model simulation. J. Phys. Oceanogr. 33(1): 313-326.

Appendix A-ACRONYM LIST

AVHRR	Advanced Very High Resolution Radiometer
CCR	Cold Core Ring
CZCS	Coastal Zone Color Scanner
EGOM	Eastern Gulf of Mexico
EIS	Environmental Impact Statements
ERS	European Remote Sensing
GOES	Geostationary Operational Environmental Satellite
GOM	Gulf of Mexico
HCMM	Heat Capacity Mapping Mission
IR	Infrared
LC	Loop Current
NASA	National Aeronautics and Space Administration
NEGOM	Northeastern Gulf of Mexico
NOAA	National Oceanic and Atmosphere Administration
SEASAT	Sea Satellite
SeaWiFS	Sea-Viewing Wide Field-of-view Sensor
SSH	Sea-Surface Height
SST	Sea-Surface Temperature
TIROS	Television Infrared Observation Satellite
TOPEX	Topography Experiment
WCR	Warm Core Ring
WFS	West Florida Shelf
WGOM	Western Gulf of Mexico

The Department of the Interior Mission

As the Nation's principal conservation agency, the Department of the Interior has responsibility for most of our nationally owned public lands and natural resources. This includes fostering sound use of our land and water resources; protecting our fish, wildlife, and biological diversity; preserving the environmental and cultural values of our national parks and historical places; and providing for the enjoyment of life through outdoor recreation. The Department assesses our energy and mineral resources and works to ensure that their development is in the best interests of all our people by encouraging stewardship and citizen participation in their care. The Department also has a major responsibility for American Indian reservation communities and for people who live in island territories under U.S. administration.

The Minerals Management Service Mission

As a bureau of the Department of the Interior, the Minerals Management Service's (MMS) primary responsibilities are to manage the mineral resources located on the Nation's Outer Continental Shelf (OCS), collect revenue from the Federal OCS and onshore Federal and Indian lands, and distribute those revenues.

Moreover, in working to meet its responsibilities, the **Offshore Minerals Management Program** administers the OCS competitive leasing program and oversees the safe and environmentally sound exploration and production of our Nation's offshore natural gas, oil and other mineral resources. The MMS **Minerals Revenue Management** meets its responsibilities by ensuring the efficient, timely and accurate collection and disbursement of revenue from mineral leasing and production due to Indian tribes and allottees, States and the U.S. Treasury.

The MMS strives to fulfill its responsibilities through the general guiding principles of: (1) being responsive to the public's concerns and interests by maintaining a dialogue with all potentially affected parties and (2) carrying out its programs with an emphasis on working to enhance the quality of life for all Americans by lending MMS assistance and expertise to economic development and environmental protection.

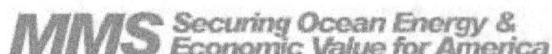